EVERYTHING HAPPENS
FOR A REASON

"With grace, wisdom, and humor, Bowler (*Blessed*), a divinity professor at Duke University, tells of her cancer diagnosis and subsequent treatment in a way that pierces platitudes to showcase her resilience in the face of impending death. . . . Bowler's lovely prose and sharp wit capture her struggle to find continued joy after her diagnosis. This poignant look at the unpredictable promises of faith will amaze readers."

—*Publishers Weekly* (starred review)

"Bowler writes with the inimitable urgency of someone staring down the gun barrel of terminal illness. As a scholar who has spent a decade studying Christian 'health and wealth' culture, she also brings the sympathy of a self-reflective researcher who understands now more than ever what her subjects really want. . . . This is the gospel promise—prosperity of the heart. And hers, captured in her memoir, is rich indeed."

—*Christianity Today*

"Throughout, [Kate Bowler] delivers raw emotion, realistic description, and candid assessments. . . . An inspiring story of finding faith—in God, in family, and in oneself—while walking close to the Valley of the Shadow of Death." —*Kirkus Reviews*

"A beautiful book . . . [Bowler's] scholarly background brings depth and unique insight to this book."

—*Patheos*

"I felt Kate was writing to me as a friend as she tries to sort out the many conflicting thoughts and feelings she's had in the year that followed her diagnosis. . . . I was deeply moved by this slim book."

—*Los Banos Enterprise*

"Kate Bowler's memoir is a meditation on sense-making when there's no sense to be made, on letting go when we can't hold on, and on being unafraid even when we're terrified. And it happens to be hilarious. Above all, though, this is a love letter to life, and it's gorgeous."

—LUCY KALANITHI, MD, FACP
clinical assistant professor of medicine
Stanford University School of Medicine

"Get to know [Kate Bowler]; you'll be glad you did for the rest of your life."　　　　—*Shawagunk Journal*

"I fell hard and fast for Kate Bowler. Her writing is naked, elegant, and gripping—she's like a Christian Joan Didion. Her spirit and perspective are so beautiful that halfway through I closed the book, turned to my wife and said: 'I have to call someone to find out how this ends. I need to know before I keep reading if she's okay.' I don't think Kate wrote *Everything Happens for a Reason* to save anybody: she was just telling the truth about her life. Regardless, I left Kate's story feeling more present, grateful, and a hell of a lot less alone. And what else is art for? *Everything Happens for A Reason* is art in its highest form, and Kate Bowler is a true artist—with the pen, and with her life."

—GLENNON DOYLE, author of the
#1 *New York Times* bestseller *Love Warrior*
and president of Together Rising

"The Kate you will come to know in this book is 100 percent real: honest, brave, holy, ridiculous, profane, hilarious, human—her fierce and beautiful words will make you ugly-cry and laugh out loud inappropriately in public places, and they will make you long for the courage to tell the truth about your life. If you pay close enough attention, you might even turn the last page and actually do it—actually tell your truth. And your life will change."

—AMY K. BUTLER, senior minister,
The Riverside Church

"This is a beautifully written, intelligent, soulful book. Kate's story makes room for anger, for love, for faith, for despair, for prayer, and for silence.

This story feels true, in the deepest way, and is necessary reading for all of us who long to walk faithfully and honestly through the darkest and most desolate of seasons."

—SHAUNA NIEQUIST, *New York Times* bestselling author of *Present Over Perfect* and *Bread & Wine*

"Kate Bowler has stage 4 cancer, and she faces it with courage and questions. In this profound memoir she searches for answers with intelligence, honesty, and a wonderfully wry humor. She comes to the simplest conclusion of all: "Life is beautiful. Life is hard." Accepting these two truths side by side can change the way we live. As ordinary an act as making coffee becomes luminous with gratitude, and gratitude is its own kind of prayer. This is a book for all of us who have sought meaning in catastrophe, and needed a way to live on."

—ABIGAIL THOMAS, author of *A Three Dog Life*

"Belongs on the shelf alongside other terrific books about this difficult subject, like Paul Kalanithi's *When Breath Becomes Air* and Atul Gawande's *Being Mortal*."

—BILL GATES

EVERYTHING HAPPENS

FOR A REASON

Everything Happens for a Reason

AND OTHER LIES I'VE LOVED

Kate Bowler

RANDOM HOUSE · NEW YORK

2019 Random House Trade Paperback Edition

Copyright © 2018 by Kate Bowler
Reading group guide copyright © 2019 by Penguin Random House LLC

All rights reserved.

Published in the United States by Random House, an imprint and
division of Penguin Random House LLC, New York.

RANDOM HOUSE and the HOUSE colophon are
registered trademarks of Penguin Random House LLC.

RANDOM HOUSE READER'S CIRCLE & Design is a registered
trademark of Penguin Random House LLC.

Originally published in hardcover in the United States by Random House,
an imprint and division of Penguin Random House LLC, in 2018.

LIBRARY OF CONGRESS CATALOGING-IN-PUBLICATION DATA
NAMES: Bowler, Kate, author.
TITLE: Everything happens for a reason : and other lies I've loved /
Kate Bowler.
DESCRIPTION: New York : Random House, [2018]
IDENTIFIERS: LCCN 2017011466 | ISBN 9780399592089 (trade paperback) |
ISBN 9780399592072 (ebook)
SUBJECTS: LCSH: Bowler, Kate,—Health. | Colon (Anatomy)—Cancer—
Patients—United States—Biography. | Cancer—Patients—Family
relationships. | Christian life. | BISAC: BIOGRAPHY &
AUTOBIOGRAPHY / Personal Memoirs. | BIOGRAPHY &
AUTOBIOGRAPHY / Medical. | RELIGION / Christian Life /
Death, Grief, Bereavement.
CLASSIFICATION: LCC RC280.C6 B68 2018 |
DDC 362.19699/40092 [B]—dc23
LC record available at https://lccn.loc.gov/2017011466

Printed in the United States of America on acid-free paper

randomhousebooks.com
randomhousereaderscircle.com

246897531

Book design by Barbara M. Bachman

ZACH, MY DARLING,

I CAN SEE NOW HOW MY BEAUTIFUL LIFE

WAS ALWAYS FOR YOU.

CONTENTS

....

CONTENTS

PREFACE

············

There's a branch of Christianity that promises a cure for tragedy. It is called by many names, but most often it is nicknamed the "prosperity gospel" for its bold central claim that God will give you your heart's desires: money in the bank, a healthy body, a thriving family, and boundless happiness.

I grew up on the prairies of Manitoba, Canada, surrounded by communities of Mennonites. I learned at my Anabaptist Bible camp about a poor carpenter from Galilee who taught that a good life was a simple one. Though most Mennonites abandoned bonnets and buggies long ago, they kept their concerns about the greediness of modern life. Everyone had a grandpa who once ruined a gleaming new car by painting the bumpers black to hide the chrome and knew that the most holy words found outside of the Scriptures were "I got it on sale." But when I was eighteen or so, I started hearing stories about a different kind of faith with a formula for success, and by twenty-five I was traveling the country interviewing the prosperity gospel's celebrities. Eventually, I wrote the first history of the movement from beginning to end.

I spent years talking to televangelists who claimed spiritual guarantees for how to receive divine money. I held hands with people in wheelchairs praying at the altar to be cured. I thought I was trying to understand how millions of North Americans had started asking God for more. How they seemed to want permission to experience the luxuries of life as a reward for good behavior. After all, the movement was best known in popular culture for Jim and Tammy Faye Bakker, the de facto King and Queen of 1980s televangelism. Their media empire toppled when Jim was convicted of financial fraud, and the scandal cemented in most people's minds the idea that the prosperity gospel was fundamentally about gold faucets, thick mink coats, and matching his-and-her Mercedes Benzes.

And I did discover that the prosperity gospel encourages people (especially its leaders) to buy private jets and multimillion-dollar homes as evidence of God's love. But I also saw the desire for escape. Believers wanted an escape from poverty, failing health, and the feeling that their lives were leaky buckets. Some people wanted Bentleys but more wanted relief from the wounds of their past and the pain of their present. People wanted salvation from bleak medical diagnoses; they wanted to see God rescue their broken teenagers or their misfiring marriages. They wanted talismans to ward off the things that go bump in the night. They wanted a modicum of power over the things that ripped their lives apart at the seams.

The prosperity gospel is a theodicy, an explanation for the problem of evil. It is an answer to the questions that take our lives apart: Why do some people get healed and some people don't? Why do some people leap and land on their feet while others tumble all the way down? Why do some babies die in their cribs and some bitter souls live to see their great-grandchildren? The prosperity gospel looks at the world as it is and promises a solution. It guarantees that faith will always make a way.

I would love to report that what I found in the prosperity gospel was something so foreign and terrible to me that I was warned away. But what I discovered was both familiar and painfully sweet: the promise that I could curate my life, minimize my losses, and stand on my successes. And no matter how many times I rolled my eyes at the creed's outrageous certainties, I craved them just the same. I had my own prosperity gospel, a flowering weed grown in with all the rest.

Married in my twenties, a baby in my thirties, I won a job at my alma mater straight out of graduate school. I felt breathless with the possibilities. Actually, it's getting harder to remember what it felt like, but I don't think it was anything as simple as pride. It was certainty, plain and simple, that God had a worthy plan for my life in which every setback would also be a step forward. I wanted God to make me good and make me faithful, with just a few shining accolades along the way. Anything would do if hardships were only detours on my long life's journey. I believed God would make a way.

I don't believe that anymore.

ONE MOMENT I WAS a regular person with regular problems. And the next, I was someone with cancer. Before my mind could apprehend it, it was there—swelling to take up every space my imagination could touch. A new and unwanted reality. There was a before, and now there was an after. Time slowed to a pulse. *Am I breathing?* I wondered. *Do I want to?*

Every day I prayed the same prayer: *God, save me. Save me. Save me. Oh, God, remember my baby boy. Remember my son and my husband before you return me to ashes. Before they walk this earth alone.*

I plead with a God of Maybe, who may or may not let me collect more years. It is a God I love, and a God that breaks my heart.

Anyone who has lived in the aftermath of something like this knows that it signifies the arrival of three questions so simple that they seem, in turn, too shallow and too deep.

> Why?
> God, are you here?
> What does this suffering mean?

At first those questions had enormous weight and urgency. I could hear Him. I could almost make out an answer. But then it was drowned out by what I've now heard a thousand times. "Everything happens for a reason" or "God is writing a better story." Apparently God is also busy going around closing doors and opening windows. He can't get enough of that.

———

THE WORLD OF CERTAINTY had ended and so many people seemed to know why. Most of their explanations were reassurances that even this is a secret plan to improve me. "God has a better plan!" "This is a test and it will make you stronger!" Sometimes these explanations were peppered with scriptures like "We know that for those who love God all things work together for good" (Romans 8:28). Except that the author, Paul, worshipped God with every breath until his body was dumped in an unmarked grave. But I knew what they were saying. It would be nice if catastrophes were divine conspiracies to undo what time and unfaithfulness had done to my wandering soul.

Other people wanted to assure me that what I'd had was enough. "At least you have your son. At least you've had an amazing marriage." I had been stripped down to the studs, and everything of worth I had accumulated was being appraised with a keen eye.

I became certain that when I died some beautiful moron would tell my husband that "God needed an angel," because God is sadistic like that.

This is what I thought about sometimes. What people

would say to the man with sandy hair and eyes I had loved since we were fifteen and thought we would never die.

I DON'T THINK I knew enough about longing ten years ago, when I started investigating the prosperity gospel. I had just bought a little house with the man I love—filled it with books, IKEA furniture, and a soft dog with legs as stout as soup cans. I was steeped in the lore of eternal youth. My life was something I could mold, or at least correct with a surge of determination. It was the same unlimited confidence that the prosperity gospel calls "victory." (And I might have chalked up my successes to my own hard work and a little luck.) Nothing was broken yet that could not be fixed. But what gives the prosperity movement breadth and depth for many is its thorough accounting for the pain of life, and for the longing we have for restoration. Those Americans trapped in failing bodies or broken relationships or the painful possibility that their lives might never be made whole can turn to this message of hope. If it is a game—with rules for success that anyone can use—then maybe they can win.

I wish this were a different kind of story. But this is a

book about befores and afters and how people in the midst of pain make up their minds about the eternal questions: Why? Why is this happening to me? What could I have done differently? Does everything actually happen for a reason? If I accept that what is happening is something I cannot change, can I learn how to let go?

EVERYTHING HAPPENS

FOR A REASON

CHAPTER I

Diagnosis

I HAD LOST ALMOST THIRTY POUNDS BY THE TIME I was referred to a gastrointestinal surgeon at Duke University Hospital. Every few hours I doubled over from a stabbing pain in my stomach. This had happened so often over the last three months that I had developed a little ritual for it: reach for the nearest wall with the right hand, clutch my stomach with the left hand, close my eyes, keep perfectly silent. When the pain subsided, I would reach into my purse, take a swig from a giant bottle of antacid, stand up straight, and resume whatever I was doing without comment. It was a little creepy to watch, I'm sure, but it was the best I could do at pretending for so long. Now I was tired of pretending. I eyed the surgeon warily as he came into the small examining room where my husband, Toban, and I waited. He sat down heavily on his stool, sighing as if already annoyed.

Then he said, "Well, I looked at your latest tests and they don't tell us anything conclusive."

"I don't understand," I protested. "I thought the last test suggested that it was probably my gallbladder."

"It's not entirely clear," he said in a hard voice.

"So you're not prepared to operate."

"Look, there is nothing to suggest that we are going after the right thing. I can take out your gallbladder and you might be in the same pain you're in today. Plus the pain and inconvenience of a surgery."

I sighed. "I don't know how to get you, or anyone, to pay attention. I've been to all your specialists, but I have been in a crazy amount of pain for three months now, and I can't keep doing this."

"Look," he said, as if having to start all over again. "We're at the squishy end of an already squishy diagnosis." He throws it back at me, nonchalant. "Again, I can take it out, but I don't know what you want me to say."

"I want you to say that you're not going to rule out the gallbladder surgery and just send me back out there with everyone else! No one is trying to help me solve this, and *I can't take it anymore*!" I could hear the desperation leaking out.

"I'm sorry you feel that way," he said. We sat there glaring at each other.

"I'm not leaving," I said loudly. "I am *not leaving* until you send me for another test."

"Okay. Fine," he said, and he rolled his eyes.

"Okay."

He wrote a note to authorize a CT scan, and I felt only relieved annoyance. They would find something simple and that would be the end of it. I'd just have to schedule my life around a surgery, nothing major.

I AM AT THE OFFICE, pacing at my treadmill desk and flipping through my latest research, when my phone rings.

"Hello, this is Kate."

It's Jan from the doctor's office. She has a little speech prepared, but my mind is zeroing in and out. I can hear that she is talking, but I can't make out the words. It is not my gallbladder, I catch that much. But now it is everywhere.

"What's everywhere now?" I ask.

"Cancer."

I listen to the buzz of the phone.

"Ms. Bowler." I absentmindedly put it back up to my ear.

"Yes?"

"We're going to need you to come in to the hospital right away."

"Sure, sure."

I need to call Toban.

"Ma'am?"

"No, sure. I get it. I'll be right there."

"I'll send someone down to the lobby to get you.

"Ma'am?"

"Sure, sure," I say, almost inaudibly. "I have a son. It's just that I have a son."

There is a long silence.

"Yes," she says, "I'm sorry." She pauses. I picture her, standing near an office phone riffling through charts. Likely there are more people to call. "But we're going to need you to come in."

"Is GOD GOOD? Is God fair?"

A hulking Norwegian asked me this once in the line at my college cafeteria.

"I think so," I said. "But it's seven A.M. and I'm starving." But now I wonder. Does God even care?

One of my favorite stories told by prosperity preachers comes from one of the original televangelism duos, Gloria Copeland and her husband, Kenneth. Gloria, who, even at seventy-something, looks like a glamour-puss real estate agent, and her husband, a true Texan, who always looks like he has strolled in after a leisurely day at the ranch. For decades, they have saturated prime-time television and the Christian bookstore shelves with teachings on living the abundant life. They don't expect God simply to be fair—they expect God to rain down blessings. So when a tornado threatened to destroy their home, said Gloria, they crept in the night to their porch to face down the storm. They prayed loud and long that God would protect their property and, for good measure, commanded God to protect their neighbors' houses, too. And so, they said, the storm turned and went another way.

It is an image I cannot forget: two of the world's wealthiest Christians shaking their fists at the sky, protesting to the God of Fair.

After all, what father, when his child asks for bread, would give him a stone?

Fairness is one of the most compelling claims of the

American Dream, a vision of success propelled by hard work, determination, and maybe the occasional pair of bootstraps. Wherever I have lived in North America, I have been sold a story about an unlimited horizon and the personal characteristics that are required to waltz toward it. It is the language of entitlements. It is the careful math of deserving, meted out as painstakingly as my sister and I used to inventory and trade our Halloween candy. In this world, I deserve what I get. I earn my keep and keep my share. In a world of fair, nothing clung to can ever slip away.

I GOT MARRIED AT twenty-two, when I was especially dumb. I wasn't dumb to marry Toban, exactly, because that ended up being one of the most sensible things I've ever done. But I was probably pretty dumb because I didn't yet realize that Toban was one of those great investment pieces that increase in value but seem like overkill. He was like beachfront property when I probably could have settled for a suburban condo. At the time, however, I mostly thought about how beautiful he was, how great he was at explaining the finer points of skateboarding, and how he would never lose his hair.

Now he rushes into my office and throws his arms around my neck, and all my words are pouring out.

"I have loved you forever. I have loved you forever. Please take care of our son."

"I will! I will!" he cries, and I know it is true. But the truth is not going to help us anymore.

I call my parents on the walk to the hospital, but I have to stop and lean against a high stone wall for a minute. Toban puts his hand on my back to steady me. We are both gone, gone, gone somewhere else, flitting back and forth between now and where we used to be.

I tell my parents they need to find a place to be together and sit down, that I have been told that I have cancer and that it doesn't look good for me.

"You need to give Zach to us! You have to change your will!" my mom blurts out, her voice shaking. I have been, coincidentally, drawing up a living will for my life insurance policy, a policy I will be denied because they will find out that I have cancer and reject the claim, a bet they no longer want to take. But right now my mother is confused. Her child is dying and suddenly, so is the whole world. She is desperate to salvage what is left of my life: my son.

"Toban will keep living, Mom. Zach can stay with him," I say gently.

"Right . . . right . . . I'm sorry. Oh, honey, I'm sorry," she says, and I can tell she is resolved to be my rock, but she is crying. They are on a trip to Toronto to see my sister Amy, and now they will scatter in the winds and find me. I will see my dad in the hospital when he strides in moments before my surgery. He will take my hand in one hand and stroke my hair with the other. This is my father, the impervious giant, who will never cry about my diagnosis. He will not allow it the dignity of defining a damn thing about his daughter and her future.

I call my sisters, and they dutifully sit. Our words feel garbled, burning hot with love. My next call finds my friend Katherine in the bleachers of a Vanderbilt football game, and she will immediately get into the car, a state away, screaming into the windshield. When I wake up from surgery she will be there, and my foggy brain will not recall that I never asked her to come. She knew I needed her. She will sleep in the hospital chair beside me, pretending it is comfortable, and using her no-nonsense voice with the nurse who won't bring me ice chips.

But for now I am sitting in a hospital room, before surgery, somewhere in the maze of Duke University

Hospital, staring down at my hands folded on my lap. A blue hospital gown is folded crisply on the bed beside me and machines chirp everywhere like crickets. I am alone for the first time since my diagnosis a few hours before, and the day is unfolding with brutal swiftness. Toban has raced home to tell Zach's indomitable nanny about what is happening, and all my family is still in transit, and I can't do anything but sit staring down at my dress, white with bright flowers and flouncy the way I like it. I love this dress. I can't take it off. I need it for teaching.

My friends Jonathan and Beth arrive. Jonathan races through the door and pulls me into a bear hug. They plunk themselves down on my hospital bed and turn to me with looks of compassionate dismay.

"I'm going to need for you to burn this," I say, finally, gesturing exasperatedly to my dress. "I can't see it again. That life is over." I am oscillating between hysteria and an executioner's humor. "I'm just the luckiest girl in the world," I say with mock enthusiasm before my mind skips to Zach long enough to send me into racking sobs. I double over crying. I squeeze my eyes closed and try to shut out the world.

"I just don't," I keep saying. "I just don't know what to do." The only things that feel real are their hands patting my back and the hospital sheets against my face. "I just don't know what to do."

"Die," says Beth in a quiet voice.

I don't know if it was a question or a fact, but I stop crying. Her word is a cliff, and I can see all the way down. Jonathan starts to reassure me, to fill the void and remake the world as it was, but all I can think of is her single word. *Die.* It is impossible. It is an impossible thought. I thought this life was only getting started, but now I am supposed to contemplate its sudden conclusion. I am supposed to imagine the end of my whirling mind, the slowing of my breath, a sunken vessel where my heart now beats. But, worse, it would be the conclusion of this thing I have built—a family.

I have had two perfect moments in my life. The first was running down the aisle with Toban on our wedding day, and we burst through the church doors and stood, breathless, alone as husband and wife, gazing at each other like complete idiots. And the other was when they put Zach in my arms for the first time and we looked at each other like it was a conspiracy of mutual adoration. These are my Impossible Thoughts. These are my Can't-Live-Withouts. I cannot picture a world where I am not theirs. Where I am simply gone.

Jonathan and Beth pray for me for a long time and put their hands on my head to bless me and kiss my wet cheeks before leaving, but not before I get Beth to wait a minute. I pull off my dress and put on the gown, clumsily knotting the ties at my back as she helps me. I hand her the dress. She knows what to do.

CHAPTER 2

Object Lesson

MY BODY HAD FAILED ME BEFORE. I WAS twenty-eight and working on my dissertation, a book-length treatment of the prosperity gospel and the final step on my way to being a professor, when one afternoon my fingers suddenly slowed and then stopped at the keyboard. I had spent long hours at the computer, but nothing seemed to warrant this surreal limpness, which extended from my shoulders to my fingertips. My arms had a limited battery life, able to hold things or write a letter one minute and then peter out the next. In the middle of a car ride, I would suddenly be unable to grip the steering wheel anymore. Shaking people's hands was fast becoming the most awkward moment of any day. Oh, hello there. Don't mind the fact that I don't seem to be gripping your hand, but that you are expertly moving my arm up and down.

By day, I had to make endless accommodations for the weakness in my arms in the way I answered email, graded papers, chopped ingredients for dinner, and went to the gym. I spent hours in the bathtub soaked in Epsom salts. I cried in the shower when I thought Toban was upstairs. Sometimes I gave up and put both arms in slings or braces and let them hang there like the world's most awkward conversation pieces. What can you do with only sporadic use of your arms? Life had become an obstacle course of things to be overcome to the sound of a ticking clock.

But by night, when my research into prosperity churches came to life in healing revivals, church services, and interviews in the pews, my arms were not just a hindrance. They were an object lesson. It wasn't only that I couldn't take notes nearly as well and I had to record things, only for them to be painstakingly transcribed later by voice dictation. But if you had seen me there, you would have witnessed a girl in double arm braces at a healing crusade swarmed by teachers, evangelists, healers, and prophets like moths to a flame. People wanted to see me pushed up to the stage to be healed by a celebrated Man of God or brushed to the side with teams of women touching my arms, my back, my head, and laboring over me in prayer. Sometimes I received an invitation to a quiet room to go over a checklist of sins I might have committed that would have opened the door to the ministrations of demons with names like Python, Sitri, and Vassago. What or who, my helpers wanted to know, was squeezing the life out of me? They took spiritual inventories, paging through my life and taking out events one by one for examination. Was this it? What darkness could God's light expose?

In a spiritual world in which healing is a divine right, illness is a symptom of unconfessed sin—a symptom of a lack of forgiveness, unfaithfulness, unexamined attitudes, or careless words. A suffering believer is a puzzle to be solved. What had caused this to happen? As I walked around with slings or braces on my arms, I heard whispers and caught looks, some sympathetic, some disapproving, some gravely concerned. In the small church where I did most of my research, I knew I was loved. I was prayed for. I was ministered to. But when, week after week, I returned with the same droop in my arms and weakness in my hands, I thought I saw their lips close and their arms cross, and I felt like faithlessness personified.

Over the next six months I visited more than thirty-five doctors to try to make sense of what was happening to me. My first appointment was disheartening.

"I think your injury is . . ." The doctor paused, turning to the physician he had brought in for consultation. They shared a long silence between them.

"Well," continued the other, "it can be common in women who share a certain size."

One of the doctors had been, unconsciously, miming the shape of breasts on his own chest for the last few seconds. I was ready to get to the end of this as quickly as possible.

"When a woman of your, um, proportions does too much yoga, then it can create certain kinds of injuries, nerve entrapment in your chest here and here," he said, pointing. "Which explains the numbness you're feeling in your arms. So ease up on the yoga!" he said with a chuckle.

I stuffed my paperwork into my backpack as quickly as possible and scooted out the door. I rarely do yoga, and I certainly was not—what's the polite word here?—encumbered.

"That's the third yoga injury we've seen like that this week!" I heard one say to the other before I shut the door behind me. A veritable epidemic of well-endowed yogis.

I WAS SAD AND ANGRY in equal measure most of the time. I would be angry at my arms and then I'd start to cry. I was constantly stewing over daily advice from friends and strangers who spied my slings and warmly recommended that I get carpal tunnel surgery. And when I sat down to work, I usually worried that my frustrated crying was going to short-circuit my laptop. There was nothing close to strength left in my arms, and I had a three-hundred-page dissertation to write. Every day I tried voice dictation software, but it skipped all over the paragraph and garbled most of the words. "Prosperity gospel" always read "perspiring gospel" but "THIS COMPUTER IS RUINING MY LIFE!" always seemed to come out perfectly. Eventually my creeping depression convinced Toban and my mother and father that I should move back home to Canada for a month so my professor parents could pretend they didn't have jobs and help me full-time. And they did— they took the dissertation down by dictation. Word for word. I sat on the couch surrounded by books and tried to arrange my ideas into sentences, and my mom or dad sat across from me pretending that each thought was riveting. Apart from that, we watched *Law & Order* episodes and ate Chinese takeout.

My body was failing me, failing all of us. Pain rippled through my limp arms. I was no longer proof of anything that testified to the glory of God, at least not in the eyes of the people around me. I was nothing like a sign and a wonder. Instead, I was living in my parents' basement, and I simmered with resentment. Wasn't I better than this? "I used to be shiny," I said to a friend with a sour laugh. "I really was pretty shiny at one point."

If you ask people in the prosperity movement how they know their lives are headed in the right direction, they talk a lot about proof. The lame will walk. The blind will see. Bills will be paid. Wives will drive gleaming cars. Children will put on neatly pressed clothes with the price tags still popping out of their collars, all evidence of who God loves. It was even the theme song for prosperity teacher Frederick Price's television show—"Evidence! Evidence! Do you need it?" sang the choir. The gospel would prove itself. But I longed to prove it too.

There is something so American about the "show-and-tell" of our daily lives. A big house means you work hard. A pretty wife means you must be rich. A subscription to *The New York Times* shows you must be smart. And when you're not sure, there will always be bumper stickers to point out who has the honor roll student and who finished a marathon. America likes its shopping malls big and its churches even bigger, and every Starbucks in every lobby proves that Jesus cares about brewing the best.

Sometimes I saw this idea under the banner of family values. It was in the way women boasted about their fat-cheeked babies and their little boys in bow ties. It was in the way the pastor displayed his wife and child in the front row and asked his little Jennifer to sing the solo: "Isn't she talented, folks?" It was in the way people bought tidy mansions with extra guest rooms in case a refugee sponsored by the church needed to stay a night. Christmas cards were prosperity gospels writ miniature, stacks of pictures of a family in matching denim sitting on lightly distressed couches in fields of waving wheat. Does every field in America have a photo couch? But I was taken with the white light brightening their smiles as they turned to each other and laughed. They were the good news.

Some bodies can't bear up under this regime of divine perfection. A friend of mine looked at his newborn daughter, dewy from birth, and could not acknowledge what he saw with his own eyes. She was plump and pink with the lightly hooded eyes of a perfect child, but a perfect child with Down syndrome. Despite all the love in his heart, or perhaps because of it, he could not say those words aloud. Down syndrome. And that sliver of iron became a commitment never to proclaim, never to "negatively confess," that his baby girl was anything less than typical. He began to believe that the God of all that is whole and complete would make his daughter so, even if it was not until Judgment Day, when Jesus came through the clouds.

What would it mean for Christians to give up that little piece of the American Dream that says, "You are limitless"? Everything is not possible. The mighty Kingdom of God is not yet here. What if *rich* did not have to mean *wealthy,* and *whole* did not have to mean *healed*? What if being people of "the gospel" meant that we are simply people with good news? God is here. We are loved. It is enough.

I received this friend's Christmas card in the mail not long after his daughter was born and stared at it on the fridge. The sun shone behind their heads, upturned in laughter, the baby on his lap, a gaggle of children hanging off of their mother. I exhaled slowly. I suddenly longed to have the strength to pick that baby up and hold her eye to eye, so I could say the words that I longed to hear: "You are perfect, my darling, just as you are. You are the gospel."

THAT WAS THE CHRISTMAS when I sat across from yet another doctor, a small man leaning into a desk littered with papers, who made it quite clear that he was terribly important and, as far as I was concerned, the final word. He asked me questions, but mostly he seemed preoccupied by the sheer number of doctors I'd seen. He sounded skeptical, as if all those doctors should have amounted to a cause already.

"I believe that your symptoms are psychosomatic. So all I can recommend is a good psychologist," he said firmly.

"You think these are invented symptoms resulting from mental problems?" I asked in astonishment. "My arms stopped working because I used them too much while writing my dissertation, and now we just have to figure out why."

I steamed. He might have been describing a complicated psychosomatic disorder that I have seen with my own eyes. A father dies and suddenly his daughter cannot move her legs. A schoolchild is petrified and suddenly feels his throat close up, unable to squeak out a word. It can happen and it can last for months, years. But I don't think that's what he was seeing. He saw an insignificant young woman with floppy arms unable to write, and I saw a doctor who refused to put his shoulder to this problem and help me. He was my final stop on the long list of doctors I had met, and I thought he was my best hope. Now all I could see were the adult braces on his teeth and the way his lips curled around them as he told me that the stress of dissertation writing had clearly gotten to me. He jotted down in my file that I required psychological assistance. Now no one would take my physical condition seriously. *Don't help me. Nothing to see here.*

I stormed out the door as quickly as possible to keep myself from crying and giving him another excuse to think I was unstable. I strode through the hallways until I was out of sight and then slumped down on the floor to call Chelsea. Chelsea and I have spent most of our lives together, and she set in stone for me what it means to feel loved and understood. In high school she learned to forgive me for our time at the same childhood judo camp, where I accidentally became her sworn enemy by repeatedly flipping her over my eleven-year-old hip and asking her, while she was flat on her back, if she had had her Wheaties today. Long ago we realized that everything that happens to one of us happens to both of us, so we treat our lives like a tandem bicycle. Where she goes, I go, but we both look a little ridiculous.

We both grew up with unlimited hope that life was fair. But that confidence began to crumble in our hands as our twenties wore on. I lost control of my body. She lost a marriage when her husband's immigration visa didn't come through. Together, we lost faith in the whole concept of things being fair. Fair would insist that people wouldn't have to use smiley or frowny stamps to grade their students' final papers because the instructor's arm was not capable of holding a pen ("This cheerful stamp conveys that this paper makes me feel [stamps page] extremely HAPPY about your detailed thesis statement!"). Justice would grant citizenship to tired immigrants who, as children, fled silently into the dark when gunshots and thick smoke filled the village air, children hoping that no one could hear the soft padding of their bare feet in the tall grasses. Fair would mean that life rewarded the good and punished the bad, or at least pretended to.

The prosperity gospel has a very simple way of explaining why life as it is must be inherently just. As it is told, God established a set of principles that keep the world in order. Just as there are natural laws of gravity and thermodynamics, there are spiritual laws that steer the courses of lives and ensure that good things really do happen to good people. The Law of Confession activates the power of positive thoughts, drawing our desires out of the heavens and into reality. The Law of Agreement allows two or more people to harness their spirituality corporately to create an answer to prayer. The Law of the Tithe supernaturally multiplies an offering of 10 percent gross income given to the church, often with a guaranteed tenfold or hundredfold return. The number of these spiritual laws depends on who is preaching. There are the Law of First Fruits and the Law of Seed Faith and an entire Laws of Life book series by the televangelist Mike Murdock, advertised as people's "favorite book outside the Bible." It's also the same premise as anything your aunt sent you about the Oprah-endorsed book *The Secret*. (Spoiler alert: The secret is to think positively.)

Spiritual laws offer an elegant solution to the problem of unfairness. They create a Newtonian universe in which the chaos of the world seems reducible to simple cause and effect. The stories of people's lives can be plotted by whether or not they follow the rules. In this world there is no such thing as undeserved pain. There is no word for tragedy.

There was a moment in the midst of my arm debacle when I thought I had found a way out of the seemingly endless cycle of hope and disappointment. I had agreed to some kind of surgery, and while I was lying in the hospital bed, waiting to be wheeled in, the nurses ran through all the typical intake questions.

"Is there any chance you're pregnant?" one asked.

"No, I'm afraid not," I said, and looked at Toban for a hard minute. We had been hoping to start a family for several years. Each month came and went, marked only by discarded pregnancy tests and a swelling silence between us about whether we were simply unlucky. Or worse. Surgery would delay the possibility of fertility treatments in what felt like a fading season.

I returned to watching *Law & Order* on the television pegged to the hospital ceiling while Toban worked at his computer in the chair beside me. Then there was a squeal of delight and multiple gasps, and then what felt like a dozen nurses pushed aside the curtain and stood over us.

"Well, honey," said one of them, "looks like you're

not going to be going into surgery today." He looked at me knowingly until I could feel my eyes fill with tears and my heart start to race. But I couldn't say the words.

"You're pregnant!" he exclaimed, and all the nurses started clapping. Toban reached out and pulled me to him, and we could hardly believe the delighted shrieks around us. I put my hand on my stomach. This was my miracle.

We talked fast and giddy on the way home, as if the car had been pumped full of ether. We were overcome with love, love for each other, love for this baby, love for this future. By the time we had gotten home from the hospital, I had had some strong feelings about using my dad's middle name if it was a boy, and Toban was convinced that all the best girl names were taken. We were high on possibility. We dithered and fussed around the house, unable to fully concentrate on anything except when we were allowed to tell our parents.

But it had already begun. I felt something strange and ran to the bathroom. I started to scream for Toban. As I sat crouched there, everything moved around me in a blur. Toban with his arms around me. My stomach sore from deep, shaking sobs. My own rage at having fallen in love with this three-hour dream.

When we had said all we could say and I had cried all

I could cry, we stood there like fools, without language or focus. Toban finally left to make coffee, to have something to do and to hold in his hands, but I couldn't bring myself to leave the bathroom. I undressed and turned on the hot water of the shower. I stepped inside, pressed my cheek against the cool tile of the wall, and closed my eyes. I could not look down. I was nothing but blood and water.

CHAPTER 3

Magic Tricks

MY FRIEND BLAIR ONCE INVITED ME TO A "Magical Extravaganza" at the local performing arts center. When we arrived, two facts became immediately apparent: The first was that it was almost impossible to see any of the actual magic tricks from the second balcony. They looked like a blur of gloved-hand gestures coupled with music that suggested we were missing a lot of mesmerizing eye contact. The other was that magic shows need something approximating magic. In the opening act, a tent rose from the stage surrounded by a flutter of dancers. They twirled and waved their arms toward center stage for what felt like forever, but as the music crescendoed and the dancers in their final poses began to tremble, we realized that something had gone very wrong. Some kind of hidden trap had clearly malfunctioned, preventing the magicians from appearing suddenly, before our very eyes. Instead, nothing happened. Nothing except that the curtain descended to the muffled sound of two women laugh-crying into their sleeves from the second balcony.

But I have seen a different kind of magic up close. I have seen parents of an autistic child buy special earphones promised to "clear out" his ear canals and let him finally understand their adoring reassurances. I have heard accounts of parents buying their dying child a pair of shoes so that he or she might get up and walk. I have browsed through advertisements from preachers who mail out wallets with the promise that they will multiply the bills inside. I thought of them all as I handed forty dollars to my chiropractor for the special magnets that were supposed to restore strength to my arms, and then a little more money for the detoxifying footbath that was meant to pull the impurities out of my contaminated body. At some point, I started to wear a special bracelet my friend gave me that had been advertised as a conduit for positive ions, or something scientific sounding, which I wore because it made both of us feel better. I was trying everything and caring less about whether it made any sense. I just needed it to *work*.

In the study of religion, we use the word *magic* sparingly because, so often, it is employed as a cheap way of describing faiths whose supernatural forces we simply don't credit. No, that dance did not make it rain. No, that buried statue in the yard did not help you sell the house. No, that special prayer did not heal your leg. The causality seems simultaneously too direct (this action yields this exact result) and too vague, like you're pulling on a thread with nothing at the end.

By then the hundred or so times that I'd sat across from a doctor, with a pen in hand and an exasperated expression, had become a blur. All I wanted was a name for what I had, a shorthand for why I still found myself unable to type, chop vegetables for dinner, or at least fake a cartwheel on the beach. My goodness, I was beginning to feel like an insecure girlfriend: *Just tell me what's wrong with me. Is it me? It's me, isn't it?*

I was a month away from getting surgery to remove two of my ribs when I got a recommendation from a childhood friend who knew me when I was a cellist. Over the years I had seen a lot of great musicians suffer from different kinds of arm pain, and backstage the un-mistakable smell of Tiger Balm always lingered in the air. My friend is a drummer, and he mentioned that there were distinctive schools of physical therapy de-signed for musicians and dancers to address their par-ticular injuries. Within a few hours I had found the name of a local physical therapist who seemed to know something about what was happening to me.

Our first meeting was a barrage of humiliations. She looked me up and down, her head shaking no, and asked me to walk for her. Touch the wall and come back. I touched the wall and came back.

"You walk like a gorilla," she said to me on my re-turn. "No, seriously. Knuckles forward. Slightly hunched. That's all gorilla."

I laughed. I am an exceedingly loud eater and a con-summate mouth breather, so this really completed the picture.

"Now lie on this bench and breathe into this blue balloon," she said abruptly, not because she was so-cially awkward but because there were a *lot* of com-pletely random things she needed me to do. After I was done breathing into a balloon, she taught me a lot of weird reaching exercises, tested my vision through various geriatric lenses, and manually "reset" my ribs because "ribs are like the chassis of a car."

It was, by far, the weirdest appointment I had ever had, but, even so, I heard myself saying: "Do you think you can fix me?"

And I believed her when she replied, in no uncertain terms: "Yes."

She diagnosed my problem easily. I had been born with overly loose joints and, with all the sitting and typing for my dissertation, my natural asymmetry had become especially exaggerated. My body responded to this assault by seizing up around my joints, trapping nerves, and shutting down my arms. Even though she called me a gorilla, this was the woman who restored the use of my arms with a little-known school of bodywork called Postural Restoration. *Presto!* Just like that, a dark chapter of my life closed.

It was the beginning of a series of gains for me, ladders that were my escape out of the Nowhere I'd been living. I landed my dream job at a major university seminary teaching the big survey of American religion to do-gooders of all kinds. I secured a contract for my first book. The publisher even let me do my own reading for the audiobook version. This is despite the fact that, five minutes into the recording, the sound technician piped his voice into the sound booth where I was sitting, marveling at my own prose.

"Is it all . . . um . . . going to be like this?" he asked, knowing that we had weeks together of recording each chapter.

"Yes?" I replied, realizing too slowly that he wasn't offering me a compliment.

Despite being aggressively boring, I was doing splendidly. Things were, in fact, going so well that the members of the storefront prosperity church I was studying started to take notice. Two of my favorite churchwomen raised it with me.

"Well, my dear, things are going really well. *And* you're hearing these great faith messages," she said, raising one eyebrow to evoke an answer. Her name is Linda, and not only is she the most devoted woman of prayer I know, but she always smells like sweet cedarwood when she wraps me in a hug.

"It works, honey," said Valerie, a polished businesswoman and an endlessly patient answerer of questions about all things prosperity. "It really works! Just look at yourself!"

I broke into a wide smile. I was studying the prosperity gospel, but that day I *was* the prosperity gospel. I had become living proof, at last.

We have words to evaluate how likely it is that our attempts to harness the supernatural are of any use. Black cats and ladders and spilling the salt are put in a box dubbed superstition, and failed prophecies are classified as fantasies or delusions. But the prosperity gospel asks you to set aside your doubts and bet it all on God's supernatural power to reach down and remake the world according to your prayer. When everything in your body says believe, believe, believe. When you find yourself turning to your neighbor and saying: "You can't imagine what I just saw." You are not just an observer anymore, you are a witness. So then the question is always, Will it work?

A PROSPERITY-MINDED FRIEND OF mine once had a loved one die so young that he couldn't conceive of it, this flowering life snipped off at the stem. He and this friend had recently been teenagers together. One day they'd been running shoulder to shoulder down a dirt road talking about their next lacrosse game, and the next his parents were choosing among glossy woods for a coffin that would keep him in the ground. And so my friend called in all those closest and dearest to gather around the boy's coffin before burial and pray. They prayed all night, all day, and then the next, forgetting to eat or to sleep, buoyed by a confidence that he would be resurrected.

"We just couldn't believe that God wouldn't resurrect him," he told me, shaking his head in exhaustion. "We couldn't believe it. We were so certain that it couldn't be the end."

Only magic, only a miracle, could start their friend's heart. And as the hours passed in prayer, their furious love dissolved into fury at the God who'd left him cold. Didn't Jesus bring Lazarus back from the grave? Couldn't God do the same with the chilling body of a well-loved boy?

They longed for a moment of suspended reality, their Lazarus moment. The worst would be undone in the span of a prayer, their dying dreams for this boy snapping back to life. *For you, God, wouldn't it be so easy?* They would see the young man's face pinking and his hand reaching out for theirs. They would hear his voice calling through the satin and wood, asking them to help him up again, and they would slap him on the back with the gentle violence of men awkwardly trying to express their love.

"You had us scared there for a minute, buddy. We thought we'd lost you," they would say, tears spilling over their cheeks. And he might reply, hugging them a little longer than he should: "I don't know what you did, but I'm so glad it worked."

CHAPTER 4

Seasons

Toban and I spent almost ten years trying not to get pregnant because I was in school for a decade, and we were comically poor. Not poor like sweet church mice. Poor like people who worried we would get scurvy because we couldn't afford to buy oranges and then got in the habit of talking about it using pirate voices. For a long time we lived in a one-room apartment that the landlord generously called an "efficiency." Toban and I could reach into the kitchen from the living room couch, which was also the bed. And the desk. We would sit on our couch-bed-desk and watch late-night televangelism and movies we found in the student center and plan our next five-dollar date. We didn't mind deferring our dreams for a while, but then the demands of school and a twenty-thousand-dollar annual income started to make those decisions for us. We got in the habit of putting our child-rearing plans on hold for another day, a day when we would have a little house with a baby room and a decent cable package instead of an antenna. But by the time we could afford our own bungalow, we realized that getting pregnant was going to be harder than we imagined. A year went by. And then another, and we thought it might be too late.

I MADE AN APPOINTMENT for us to meet with a fertility doctor, and immediately resented every bit of paperwork leading up to our first appointment. I would read the question aloud to Toban and then exclaim: "This is none of their business!"

"It is literally their business," he replied.

"Well . . . it *shouldn't* be," I huffed. I tried to resign myself to the indecency of it all, and I missed feeling like there were details of my life that medicine's expert ears would not hear. But I could not afford any privacy. We went to the doctor and it was as I had expected: poking and prodding and waiting.

After a few appointments, Toban and I were dawdling in the car outside the fertility center one day, counting babies.

"I see absolutely *zero* babies," I said after counting the first dozen or so women going in and out. "This must be a terrible repository for babies."

"It's not a repository for babies," Toban said, laughing. "This is for potentially *making* babies. In the least sexy way possible."

I looked down at our hands, entwined on my knee.

Our doctor, Dr. Gandhi, was exhaustingly clinical, but as he started to rattle off our treatment options, he reminded me of my high school friend Ankita's dad, who used to look down at us through his spectacles and quiz us about trouble we might be up to as if it were 1965.

"Have you been joyriding, girls? Have you been necking with boys at the drive-in pictures?" The trick was to look at his glasses and not in his eyes so you didn't burst out laughing.

Dr. Gandhi was looking at me, a little disappointed, but I wasn't sure why. I didn't think the charts he gave us were particularly definitive about the problem, and the solutions were a hazy mix of needles and pills and indefinite periods of waiting. He recommended delaying any treatment and suggested that we keep an eye on hormone levels for a few months to further diagnose the problem. But the waiting was pulling me down and backward into those feelings, familiar from months of trying to solve the mystery of my arms, of exhausted unknowing. I was already tired of doctors. I was tired of waiting, I was tired of keeping my dreams on a tight leash.

For the next few months I managed the disappointment of no result with prayer and cookie dough and long periods of lying silently in the crook of Toban's arm. He'd wrap his arms around me and we'd stare at the botched drywall experiment that became the ceiling in the bungalow we rebuilt with our love and our religious determination that all construction work should be done by family members.

I had never noticed how much prosperity churches talk about waiting until I began this long season of maternal deferment. I had never noticed how many women were pushing strollers and jostling babies with smooshy cheeks until I had to regularly stand up and sing a Sunday favorite by Juanita Bynum:

> I don't mind waiting,
> I don't mind wa-it-ing.
> I don't mind waiting, on You, Lord.

She draws out the word like she has forever to wait, forever to sit with a merciful God, forever to hear God finally say: *It's time. It's time.*

Waiting is the language of Ecclesiastes: "To everything there is a season and a time to every purpose under heaven." Except that the prosperity gospel usually makes believers into farmers with "seed faith" sown in the ground, sitting in church, waiting for the rain and the harvest.

One Sunday I watched a woman grow so impatient that she called down the rain. It was the First Lady of the little prosperity church I studied, a slight woman who always sat in the front row, impassively fanning herself as her husband stirred up a fiery sermon. Then, one Sunday, she suddenly stood up and turned toward the congregation.

"Our faith requires action!" she declared with surprising strength. "We must see disease, poverty, and unanswered prayers for what they are—Satan's work. Now stand up! Stand up!" The small room shuffled to stand up, murmuring with excitement.

"Now, after I say, 'Money, cometh unto me,' you call out to God for what you are entitled to. God's blessings are already poured out for you. Now you must claim them. Claim them! Are you ready?"

"Yes!"

"*Money!*" she shouted. "Now say it with me! *Money! Cometh* unto me . . . *now!*" And with that, the First Lady began to dance. She kicked her high heels under a chair and bounced in place, reaching her arms higher and higher as she plucked invisible dollar bills from the sky. The room erupted into dance as some eighty believers, young and old, shook off their nerves and slowly joined her. It started as a murmur, as people began to speak their true hearts, and grew as their legs pumped in place and people began to shout.

"A car!"

"The green house."

They reached out for blessings visible only to them. Young mothers jostled their babies as they jumped, while elderly women waved their arms to catch what fell. Tears streamed down people's faces as they dug up their deepest desires and the losses they hoped to replace.

A husband and wife who had lost all of their children simply clutched each other with one arm each and with the other reached up to the sky.

"A baby," I said quietly, as the shouting faded and people slumped back into their seats, exhausted. A baby.

———

IN THIS SEASON OF endless postponement, Chelsea and I were so happy for other people that we were exhausted. We were so happy for Amanda that her husband made so. much. money. in whiskey sales that she could stay at home or find the most flattering angle for her selfies whenever she was sunning herself on tropical vacations. We were thrilled for Joanna that her family planning went off without a hitch and she gave birth to little Cade on exactly the day she wanted. We couldn't get enough of hearing Christine talk about the pounds flying off as she really put her mind to it. "Self-discipline, girls," she said, and we sucked our stomachs in a little more.

In fact, we were getting so good at being happy for people that we started to develop a special tone of voice, which sounded a little like a Valley Girl on helium, for people who couldn't stop telling us how easily they had found their place in the sun. Whenever I found myself saying something like "And then you went backstage with the band *again*?" I reminded myself to pull out the statement "I'm soooooooooo happy for you." It was deliciously insincere, but only Chelsea knew that, and it was a balm to my soul. I was surrounded by the world's luckiest people in a culture that doesn't believe in luck.

Oprah Winfrey is a one-woman crusade against "luck." "Nothing about my life is lucky," she has argued. "Nothing. A lot of grace, a lot of blessings, a lot of divine order, but I don't believe in luck. For me, luck is preparation meeting the moment of opportunity." Luck implies that there might have been a moment when, God forbid, good fortune might have gone next door. Luck might mean we cannot say, unbowed, with the poet William Ernest Henley: "I am the master of my fate. / I am the captain of my soul."

Nothing in me wanted to take anything away from the people I loved. But I was becoming more and more like Solomon in Ecclesiastes, pulling at dark threads. There is a time to get, and a time to lose. A time to rend, and a time to sew. But at baby showers and dinners for job promotions, I listened to the tradition anew. There is a time to speak and a time to shut your piehole.

I BELIEVED IN MAGIC ONCE.

I was playing bingo with my friends in the monstrous bingo hall of an equally monstrous casino, its tall domes studded with artificial lights, making night and day indistinguishable. There were hundreds of players in little terraces that spread down to the floor, where a man plucked numbered balls out of what looked like a giant popcorn machine. My friends and I were high rollers, each armed with a pink dabber to blot out the numbers and a three-dollar bingo card on which a single person could play not one but six whole games.

We played the first game, then the second, slowly gaining confidence in the pace and the rules. The winner of the first game was the first person to play a horizontal line. The winner of the second game was the first one to fill the square around the central numbers. And so on. But then the grand finale—blackout. The first person to blot out the entire card would win thirteen hundred dollars, the biggest cash prize of the night.

I was roughly three numbers away from winning when I began silently to pray a completely absurd prayer.

Dear Jesus, I thought, totally embarrassed. *I know you don't normally do this kind of thing, and that it would be dumb if you did. But we are really broke right now and I would love to win that money. So, if you wouldn't mind, could you help me win at . . .*

"Bingo!"

I shouted it so loudly that I startled the woman next to me.

"*Bingo!*" I yelled again, but then, seeing everyone's heads slowly turn toward me, I had a moment of doubt. "*But I could be wrong!*"

But I was right. The officiant came over with great fanfare, carrying hundred-dollar bills that he arranged in a flat pyramid in front of me and my friends, who cried with laughter after I recounted my prayer. I had prayed to God like He was a candy dispenser, and it had worked. We were converted.

I used the same words a few months later when I was locked in the bathroom holding a pregnancy test. I still hadn't had any fertility treatments, but even so, my body seemed to be working. I took one, two, then three positive pregnancy tests. Then I shouted through the door, unable to look at Toban and see the expectation in his eyes.

"*I'm pregnant!*" I yelled, trying to keep my voice as flat as possible.

Silence.

"*But I could be wrong!*" I could hear him laughing through the door.

"How can you be wrong, hon? Are those tests not very accurate?" he asked reasonably. "And what are you still doing in there?"

I was lying on the floor, effectively barricading myself in with my feet against the door. I couldn't face it. I couldn't face him. I felt like the moment I saw him everything would be real. Thank God the phone was in there with me. I dialed Chelsea's number, choked up by the impossible news. If magic was about formulas and saying the right words, I knew this wasn't magic. It was something else.

"Chelsea, you wouldn't believe it, but I think I finally got lucky."

I thought about what I had said a second too late. And we laughed so hard we had to put our phones down for a minute to retie our ponytails.

MY BODY, AS IT turned out, was not nearly as eager to bear a child as my mind was. Pregnancy hormones were loosening me up at every joint, already lax from the same condition that had caused me to feel heaviness and numbness in my arms. I was a jellyfish. As the pregnancy progressed and my hips softened, my belly hung off my ligaments like lead. The baby was safe and snug, but it was, literally, pulling me apart.

Week by week, I spent more and more time in the bathtub, floating. I slowly hoisted myself out of bed in the morning and taught classes to divinity school students all day. I teetered on my shoes in the morning, and by midday, I plopped myself on a table or a chair and taught almost face-to-face with the class. I tried to be relatable and fun, but mostly I tried to pretend that pregnancy was an uncomplicated blessing.

It was a healthy pregnancy by every standard except that I wanted to put myself in a light coma until sometime after the baby was born. *Please, anyone, surprise me with a baseball hat to the head.* The pain was a dull roar. At a faculty dinner, I looked up and realized that someone had been talking to me for quite a while.

"I'm so sorry," I said, blushing. "This baby is just so . . . loud."

People kept telling me, "Oh, you wait until the baby is born! *Then* you'll see how hard it is," and I wish now they could have seen the look on my face when I finally went into labor. Deep into the rhythm of arduous contractions, I found myself smiling.

"This is nice," I panted to my sister-in-law over the phone. "Seriously, this feels so much better."

When we arrived at the hospital, a day into hard labor that wouldn't progress, the doctor looked me up and down and suggested that we return home again.

"You don't have the look of someone in labor," she said matter-of-factly.

"Yeah, well, you're going to want to check me. I am, unfortunately, amazing at being miserable."

I had one of those deliveries that mothers shouldn't talk about because the world would, in an instant, stop having children altogether. All I will say is that labor lasted thirty-seven hours, and at many points, it was without the soothing comforts of modern medicine. But when the baby continued to go into distress, his heartbeat fluttering on the beeping monitor, the doctors decided it was time for a C-section, and many hours after they made that call, he was pulled from my body and placed into my arms.

As someone who has never had overly mushy feelings about babies, I have to say it was the most bizarre feeling I had ever had. It felt like something had pushed the reset button and my life had only begun. I should have asked for a birth certificate for myself.

What followed was a blissful year. That is the most annoying thing in the world to say, in a world full of mothers who struggle with breast-feeding, high fevers, long days, and late nights. But I can only try to redeem myself by saying that I was completely caught off guard by my outrageous happiness. I had a Zach. And a Zach suited me perfectly. He smelled like vanilla extract and cookies almost all the time, and when he didn't I sat him on a puffy waterproof cushion shaped like a frog in warm water in our farmhouse sink.

Baby Zach looked a lot like a guppy staring at me with wide, expressive eyes. He was hard to feed. Hard to entertain. Hard to put down to bed. Every time he wanted to relax, he demanded a brain-stem-loosening jiggle of his whole body up and down, up and down in order to chill out for a moment and close his eyes. Some of the photos I circulated of Zach made him look like a wizened librarian with a comb-over, his thick cardigan pulled up around his neck, but I looked at him with the delusional love of a mother who knew he was going to be beautiful. And he was.

My first book, on the prosperity gospel—my other baby—had come out only months before Zach was born, so I spent this time in that sweet postbook haze that scholars love so much. The book is out in the world, looking important and busy, while you are at home in your pajamas eating pizza. I was wrapped in a cocoon of my husband's love, my son's squawking, and the glorious façade of efficiency.

On my thirty-fourth birthday I could finally admit it to myself. I sent a thank-you to all my family and friends with a little picture of Zach, perched on his little frog in the sink, his hair sprouting up from his head like an antenna. It read:

Contrary to reports that 33 (The Jesus Year) must end badly, this was officially the best year of my life. And if anyone is a notary, we can make it official. Thanks for supporting me until I got to this, my own little prosperity gospel.

My 150-person American Christianity class caught wind of the note and sent me a giant gift basket filled with onesies and T-shirts for Zach plastered with enormous lettering that said it all: BLESSED.

CHAPTER 5

Surrender

JONATHAN AND BETH, BEARING AWAY MY DRESS, have been gone for hours, and now I lie in my hospital bed waiting for my surgery. I am counting up my time and realizing that it will not be enough, and I long for that God of Yes. I keep thinking, *I am thirty-five. I am thirty-five. I will not live out the year, and this time will not be enough. It will not be sufficient to raise a little baby to adulthood. It will not be the life that I promised to my husband. It is a poor imitation of the future I had planned. Lord, take this cancer away. Save me. Let me be a wife and mom and professor who loves you and lives to tell of your glory.* I am bargaining. I am trying to find the magic formula that lifts me out of this sterile room and back, back to the warmth of my own bed and the sound of Zach babbling over the baby monitor about Mama and tractors. But mostly tractors. *God, let me stay the mom of a boy who loves tractors.*

EVERYTHING FEELS STRANGE AND slow. On pain medication and without clocks, I can't say for sure if it is still the same day as my diagnosis, the day of my surgery, or if they are one and the same. The first indication I have that it has been two days since my diagnosis is that the church is keeping vigil. This will turn out to be one of the great advantages of working at Duke Divinity School—all my friends are pastors. My colleagues teach pastors, my friends are pastors, and my students are going to be pastors. There is a flood of pastors not only in my room but in the nearby waiting room and in the divinity school's own chapel, where the community had decided to come together and pray me through my surgery. They gathered in the warm wood sanctuary and sang hymns and read Scripture and prayed thick, layered prayers in a way that only desperate people can. When the main service ended, they came to the hospital and traded off like relay runners, each praying for me until relieved. Some are close friends and some are acquaintances, and most are much, much smarter than I am. So it pleases me to no end to find out later that the most serious scholars I have ever known— authors of weighty books and owners of many velvet smoking jackets—have cried snotty tears as they pleaded with God to extend my life. They are teaching me the first lesson of my new cancer life—the first thing to go is pride.

THE MOMENTS BEFORE I go into surgery are, comedically speaking, always a real high point for me. Over the course of my life, some of my best material has been in those pre-operating table moments, when nurses are clucking around me and a hotshot doctor is giving instructions. Before my wisdom teeth were removed, with a few drugs—okay, a lot of drugs—I grabbed someone by the collar and told them to keep the teeth. I was making a necklace for Toban. Before my emergency appendix removal, I had some solid remarks about minimizing scars for the swimsuit portion of the Miss Canada contest.

So when I tell the nurses this time that I am finally

going to hit my goal weight when this giant tumor is cut out of my colon, it gets a big response. But then I follow it up with what I have really wanted to say since I fought with this doctor about my stomach pain, when I had yelled, "I am not going back out there with everyone else," and he had rolled his eyes. He is standing beside me now, and I grab his arm, pull him toward me, and say in a low, serious voice: "I had better not die looking into your eyes." The nurses roar. I have mentally decided that when the Lifetime movie version of my life is made, the doctor will be played by Matthew McConaughey with firm instructions to always chew gum and be looking into the middle distance just past me. And I am Winona Ryder, and a thousand emotions will always flit over my perfect face.

The doctor will actually make another miracle for me, so audiences will have to grow to love him. The surgery has taken four hours instead of two, and the waiting room—filled to the brim with my friends, my colleagues, and my dad, who won't stop pacing—is sunk low with speculation that something has gone very wrong. Instead the doctor has taken the extra time to sew me back together instead of giving me a colostomy bag. He didn't have to. An hour or so before the surgery, a woman with a very calming voice had stopped by with a giant plastic bag and told me that I would be, well, going to the bathroom out of a hole in my stomach for the foreseeable future but not to worry. A *lot* of celebrities have them. And I said something deep like "Sure," because at the time, I didn't think I'd make it through the night anyway.

The way that doctors are delicately picking up and handling the words "Stage Four" suggests that I am a spaghetti bowl of cancer. And oddly, this reality has filled me with love. Love for my son. Love for my friends and family. Love for my husband, sitting beside me, squeezing my hand moments before the surgery.

"This is proof," he says, "even though I never questioned it. But the way you look at me." He stops. He can't say any more. But he knows—I hope he knows—that I have loved him since he was fifteen and put bleach spray in his blond hair to make it even blonder and wore purple tank tops that should never be spoken of.

He is the reason that, when he leaves me for a moment, I call Chelsea and my sister-in-law and give them instructions in an artificially determined voice: "You have to promise me that you will tell him to get remarried. I don't want this to be the end of both our lives."

By the time I have reached the words "Zach needs a mom," I can't say any more and they can't hear any more. They want to hear that I will fight and pull myself back from the edge. I want to hear that it is settled that my life and my love will not undo each other.

I couldn't sleep last night, and I spent the hours alone, awake, thinking through questions that are useless to me now. Why did the doctors keep sending me home in pain all summer? How could the ER doctor give me antacids and tell me that people come in with all manner of stubbed toes and little things these days? I spent the summer with bright pink Pepto-Bismol in my purse and waves of stomach pain that left me gasping. And, after all that, I got the second-least-sexy cancer, colon cancer. At least it's not rectal cancer.

But I wake up after surgery, surprised. Pleased. As I am rolled through the hallways from the operating room, I see another good friend, Chad, who drove all night from Alabama to stand beside Toban with an encouraging smile on his face.

"Oh, buddy," I apparently say to him, "of course you're here . . . that is *so* nice. . . . And you look soooooo skinny."

It is the first of many things I tell people when I am on drugs, because Drugged Kate has a lot of feelings and opinions about how people should live their lives. Mostly I try to tell my friends and family how much they mean to me but end up saying that and more.

A few hours later I am sitting with a beloved friend. "Oh, my dear one, it's time. It's time to go. You can leave your career! Yes, it's still undone. The work here is still undone. But if you stay here a bitterness is going to eat up everything I love about you. If you don't go, I will hate you forever." I say that last bit to make him laugh, because my hand is on his head and tears are trickling down both our faces. He is getting older, but he will leave town not long after this and start life over someplace new. Later, just knowing that he is happy—that people I adore can restart their lives—glues something inside of me back together.

A colleague is sitting beside me, and I am, for a reason I can't later remember, telling him what to do: "You can't be happy unless you forgive them and set them aside. There is no way around it, buddy. You have to forgive." My friend is stuck, but if he were unstuck, oh, he would conquer the world. But first he must stop carrying the weight of disappointment and comparison. I don't know why I never said that before.

I save my most terrible love for Chelsea, my rock, my friendship twin. The nurses are changing my bandages, and I have my phone pressed hot against my ear. Chelsea and I are trying to talk, but there is too much to say.

"I think I'm running out of time, honey," I say finally. "I'm not trying to be dramatic, but here's what I worry about: What if you are too?" She knows what I am saying. She is working harder than anyone I have ever known, but her selflessness has caused her to surrender too much of herself to "someday." And now someday has come, at least for me.

Whenever I have fallen apart, she has reassembled the pieces. I know she wants to reach through the phone and pull me back into our bubble, where one of us cries and the other diagnoses the problem with merciless affection.

"I have to go," I say finally. "I've got to adjust my meds." But we just sit there, clinging to goodbye, before I say at last: "Go live your life, Chels."

All these words I am tripping over are benedictions. Live unburdened. Live free. Live without forevers that don't always come. These are my best hopes for you, that you press forward at last. I don't know how to die, but I know how to press this crushing grief into hope, hope for them. It doesn't sound much like goodbye. It sounds more like this: Fare thee well, my loves.

———

PEOPLE COME TO MY BEDSIDE in the hospital, but then they go, and the beep, beep, beep of the heart rate monitor remains. This is the most alone I've ever been. I grew up surrounded by communities of Mennonites, and you're never alone when you're with them. Mennonites are people with the land in their blood and a hopeless obsession with simplicity, frugality, pacifism, and Jell-O salads. I'm not Mennonite by birth, but I attended a Mennonite church, a Mennonite Bible camp, and a Mennonite wedding—my own. I married a gorgeous, square-jawed Mennonite boy when both of us were practically teenagers and he was still mildly enchanted by my propensity for spontaneous song. But a Mennonite marriage was a rich inheritance, as I acquired enough people to fill an entire basement of folding tables covered in turkey and jiggling salads for Thanksgiving.

The best and worst parts of Mennonite culture stem from the fact that it is an exclusive club. Since they typically immigrated to the United States and Canada in huge waves, often from the same communities in southern Russia, all Mennonites come from the same stock. Where I grew up, they have one of twenty exciting last names to choose from: Dueck, Loeppky, Penner, Bark-man, Friesen, et cetera. I was often a bridesmaid in a Fricsen-Friesen wedding, and even at my own wedding rehearsal, when I asked for Mark Penner to come up to the front, three people stood up. Most people are born into the tribe and, though science has not yet proven it, I'm pretty sure they are genetically predisposed to singing in four-part harmony and making thick-braided breads and homemade jam. Mennoniteland was also the best place on earth to find a boyfriend.

But the part I miss right now is how wonderful they are at suffering together. Every Mennonite family is the bearer of a sad history kept in living memory. They make time to tell the kids about the first Canadian winters endured by their great-grandparents and proudly display a massive coffee table version of a book called *Martyrs Mirror* from the 1600s, which catalogs the grisly deaths of their ancestors. Perhaps that is the most oddly comforting thing about joining the Mennonite club: they insist that suffering never be done alone. People tell stories about "our" suffering, "our" town, "our" community. When some Mennonite factions objected to, say, English-language instruction in the classroom, whole communities uprooted and moved together to a new place to start afresh. They might be the most quarrelsome group I have ever studied. I once read an entire year's worth of debates over the continued use of a hymnal they already liked. But I love their goal—unanimity. They will live and die together.

I am starting to worry that I will die here, apart, away from my home among the Mennonites of Canada, away from that delicious feeling of being folded into something. It was a feeling that began for me at Thanksgiving years ago, when I saw that Toban's Grandma Penner had put my name in black ink on a little place card on my plate. Toban and I were only dating, but there I was—written into their lives on a note card she kept year after year. Suddenly, the house seemed alive. I could hear the gentle ribbing of the men comparing notes on cars they had wrecked and see Toban's aunts, cousins, and sisters setting down a dozen pies on the Ping-Pong table. Grandma Penner called me over and, with her wrinkled hands, showed me how to roll the buns into thick pull-apart sheets. After we all sat down to the folding tables and sang the doxology, one of the young wives of a second cousin looked at my place card.

"Pen, huh?" she asked wryly.

I smiled.

"That's fantastic," she said, with a laugh. "You're in.

My grandma took one look at my brother's girlfriend and whispered to me, 'Let's put this one down in pencil.'"

But not everything can be done together. Toban is sitting beside me on the hospital bed and I'm trying to explain it to him, the way that everyone acts like one day I will fly away. A new pair of wings will suddenly sprout on my back and my feet will lift off the ground. I will wave goodbye as I am taken up, up into the clouds.

"It's not like that," I tell Toban. "I will not fly away."

Toban is looking at me with that studied expression he gets when he doesn't understand but he knows it is the wrong time to ask a question. He leans toward me and takes both my hands.

"I will not fly away," I repeat, my speech garbled with emotion. I keep thinking about this boy I heard about, a teenage boy in his final days of dying from cancer. He kept choking until his doctor finally figured out what he wanted. He wanted one last, hard cry, but his lungs were so filled with fluid that he couldn't catch his breath. So the nurses were called and they managed to slowly drain his lungs so the boy could sob until that one horrible and satisfying full stop.

"I don't know how to explain it, Toban. It's like we're

all floating on the ocean, holding on to our own inner tubes. We're all floating around, but people don't seem to know that we're all sinking. Some are sinking faster than others, but we're all sinking!"

I keep having the same unkind thought—*I am preparing for death and everyone else is on Instagram*. I know that's not fair—that life is hard for everyone—but I sometimes feel like I'm the only one in the world who is dying.

"We're all sinking, slowly, but one day, while everyone watches, I will run out of air. I am going to go under." Even explaining it, I feel more and more frantic. "There will be a day when I can't take my next breath. And I will drown."

I can picture it so clearly. People talk about heaven like it's a hop, a skip, and a jump. A veil between heaven and earth will part and I will pass through it.

The promise of heaven to me is this: someday I will get a new set of lungs and I will swim away.

But first I will drown.

EVERY MORNING I LIVE the same moment. I can hear Zach over the baby monitor, squawking and mewing, and murmuring the first words, "Mama! Papa! Da-doo!" which, roughly translated, mean, "Mother, father, tractor, save me from this prison."

It used to be the beginning of my favorite part of the day. I wake to the sounds of my son, and as I lift him out of his crib, warm milk waiting beside the change table, I have reinvented the world. I have rescued twenty pounds of chubby arms, legs, and cheeks and set him free to move about the house to identify toy tractors and bring fleece onesies back into fashion.

Ever since the diagnosis there has been a moment, in the minute between sleeping and waking, when I forget, when I have only a lingering sense that there is something I am supposed to remember. In the warmth of my bed, I am caught in webs of dreams. And then there is the flood. *I am dying. I am dying. I am my son's first goodbye.* I am not the start of a great new day. I am a bright sunset.

And then one day, I have cancer in my dreams. I am looking into the window of a perfectly average home to see another woman set the table and stoop to pick up my son. I am on a boat caught in the storm and I say to the crew in a bright voice, *Don't worry about me. I was already going to die.* I say it with such certainty, impervious to the weight of it and the sound it makes on my lips. But in the day—the real day—I am beginning to notice the expansion of this grief. My friends bear the brunt of my honesty. Chelsea starts to receive all my passwords and firm instructions about how my work should be handled. Laceye learns where all the diaries are kept that I would rather not leave for posterity. The diary of twelve-year-old Kate will be allowed to remain, because it is a daily account of what a boy named Colin was doing and I am convinced that if Colin committed a crime in 1992 and is later put on trial, my diary is so thorough that it would either convict or exonerate him.

I HAVE BEEN BACK from the hospital after surgery for two weeks and am slowly trying to move around but mostly sitting in every chair. So, naturally, I begin to conscript my family and whoever happens to be visiting to bring me all my books from around the house. I'm trying to decide what I can read in the time I have left. Then I give the rejects away or get my laptop and start to list them online. I spend hours on this self-appointed project, and I force my dad and my friends to sit there with me, squinting at the fine print in the first few pages of every book to find the bar codes and the ISBN numbers. My mom used to call this approach the "Giant

Mitts" for the way I can slowly squeeze people into doing what I want them to do. She meant it in a nice way, something about a happy, fluffy kind of leadership. But looking at my assembly line of workers, each behind a pile of books so high I can barely see them, I am starting to see who I still am. I am a well-oiled machine of perfect efficiency. We do this for hours and late into the night. *Why would Toban want all these books?* I ask them. *These books have always been my hobby, my thing. Wouldn't it be awful for him to have to sort through these hundreds of books?*

"LIFE IS A SERIES OF LOSSES," says my father-in-law one afternoon. We are sitting outside on the patio, where I always sit now, wrapped to my eyeballs in blankets and looking up at the sky. There is something about a ceilingless world, the slow drift of clouds, and the sound of birds that staves off the taste of fear.

"What, Dad?" I love calling him Dad. He has earned it with his gentle fix-it nature and his willingness to braid my hair on camping trips.

"Oh, I was just thinking about how, with age, it is one loss after another," he replies.

"Huh." He is right. With age we slowly lose our senses and even our pleasures, our parents and then our friends, preparing us for our own absence. An interesting thought.

"First there was racquetball," he says suddenly, jolting me back to the present.

"What?"

"I had to give up racquetball in my fifties."

"That's not exactly the kind of thing I'm worried about right now!" I yell with mock rage. He laughs and then spends the next half hour trying to remake his point until I demand that he never repeat it again and that we get coffee and a biscuit because my habits are increasingly geriatric.

Lord, save me from old people. It will become a constant refrain with my older friends that the moment one of them starts to complain about an aching hip, all the rest will slowly turn and look for my response. And I will not disappoint them.

"I'm soooooorry," I sympathize, my voice thick with sarcasm. "Is your loooooooong life becoming an encumbrance?" They are always full professors with endowed chairs and weighty accomplishments, so I suspect that they have not been properly made fun of before. But they are becoming some of my closest friends. We can sit on the same bench, quietly wondering what to do with this unwinding clock.

I have started writing letters to Zach in the quiet between naps, hospital visits, and my earnest sister-in-law fussing over how to get me to eat. Zach can sit on the bed with me, but mostly he wants to roll around, and he can't touch the tender stitches across my stomach. Not touching him is exhausting. Time has started to feel like it's getting away from us. When he gets older, will he know how I felt the moment they put him in my arms? *There was nothing like it, Zach. The nurses said that when our eyes met, I kept repeating: "It was you. It was you the whole time."*

I used to think that grief was about looking backward, old men saddled with regrets or young ones pondering should-haves. I see now that it is about eyes squinting through tears into an unbearable future. The world cannot be remade by the sheer force of love. A brutal world demands capitulation to what seems impossible—separation. Brokenness. An end without an ending.

It is one thing to abandon vices and false starts and broken relationships. I have tried to scrounge around in my life for things to improve, sins to repent of, things to give God to say, *There. I gave it all*. But it is something else entirely to surrender my family—three links in a chain. It is not mine to give. I can see the hunger in my husband's eyes as I pause for a moment at our son's crib. He is watching me as if I am fading into gray. I meet his eyes because it is all I can do. I can be gentle with that man, keep my tone soft, tuck the blankets around his bare muscled shoulders as he falls asleep. I can try to communicate, *I know. I know. The water is rising and the levees may break and it will sweep us all away. But until then, I am here. I will not let go.*

I ONCE STUMBLED INTO a prosperity megachurch expecting to find a regular service and instead found a funeral. I picked up the bulletin and saw a famous face staring back at me from the cover, smiling as he always did. I had considered him to be a kind and straightforward sort of preacher, happy to guarantee healing and prosperity because he believed in God's abundant provision with his whole heart. But he died in middle age surrounded by people—well-meaning people—clawing for the meaning of his death. Even the bulletin had to include a separate section to address the question on everyone's minds: *Why? Did he lack faith? Did he fail to live out his own teachings?* In a theological universe in which everything you do comes back to you like a boomerang—for good or for ill—those who die young become hypocrites or failures. Those loved and lost are just that, those who have lost the test of faith.

I have heard countless stories of denial in the face of death. A pastor stops a funeral to try to resurrect a young boy being put into the ground. A woman in the hospital hears her diagnosis and refuses treatment because she believes God will heal her, growing frail as her family watches in desperation. A famous healer dies after using his own ulcerated leg as a litmus test for his faith. The United States Postal Service asks a prosperity preacher to cease claiming the power to resurrect the dead. Desperate families have stopped up the flow of mail to his headquarters with coffins.

But mostly I see people who refuse to allow their loved ones to grow weary. In the waiting room, a daughter asks her elderly mother to put on her lipstick and smile before seeing the doctor. A man I know wants to call it quits on his painful gauntlet of medical treatments, but he can't bear the disappointment of his family. My nurse keeps saying, "But at least you're here now!" when reviewing the boxes I have checked on the form she has given me: Fatigue. Insomnia. Pain. Depression. There are no words that don't sound like surrender.

THERE MUST BE RHYTHMS to grief, but I do not know them.

People begin to take their turns grieving me because it can't be done all at once. Family and friends who could not be at the hospital for my operation come to stay at the house, and we start all over at the beginning. I sit outside, wrapped in the same blankets and taking in the sunshine, all my favorite people orbiting around me. My pastor takes out her Psalms and reads a little, gripping my hand. My mom cooks a lot, stocking the freezer with everything that is suggested to be anticancer. My older sister, Amy, sends treats and constant encouragement, while Maria, my younger sister, gives me her words when she can't be there, sending me poems and bits of trivia from New York, where she is working as an editor for a Catholic magazine. She has two big hopes for me: one, that I will be cured; the other, that, before it is over, I will punch the nearest inconsiderate person in the face.

I have so many fears, spoken and unspoken. When I first got my job at Duke and realized that I was going to live in the United States for some time, I made a lot of loud protestations about how *"I will not die in a foreign land!"* I also made clear that I would not die in my office, not only because that had happened before to professors (prone, as they are, to get preoccupied by their research) but also because it seemed sad, at twenty-nine, to feel exiled to the Land of Opportunity for eternity. I think back on how I casually strategized about where I would be buried, concerned that I would never be able to reconcile all the parts of my identity. A daughter who lives far from family. A friend who spends too much time at work. A wanderer but a type A planner. I wondered if I would ever be one, whole person. But now I am not hoping for completeness of any kind. All I can think of are the logistics. One night I wake up almost every hour because my mind has seized on a horrible question: Wouldn't it be a paperwork nightmare to move my body? To take me home?

When I teach pastors at the seminary where I work, I lecture them about the First Great Awakening and religious responses to the Civil War and how their political differences will ruin their next Thanksgiving if they don't learn to shut their traps. But as a historian, I have never spent any time teaching them how to perform baptisms, officiate weddings, or conduct funerals. And I have certainly never told them what to say when they visit someone who is dying and how not to sit on her couch, mouth full of cookies, and ask endless questions about how cancer treatment works. I did not tell them how few of their words are needed but how much their hands are wanted, a hand on my back as I tear up, a hand on my head for a soft prayer for healing. When I feel I am fading away, these hands prop me up and make me new. When my older colleague Frank, who lost his own adult son, found his way into my hospital room, he wrapped his strong hands around mine and said, quietly: "I wore this clerical collar to impress you. And also to get through hospital security."

The prosperity gospel understands the power of touch perhaps better than anyone except maybe Catholics, who are always making everything into something you can run through your fingers or, if it's bolted to the floor, at least take worshipful pictures next to. But prosperity believers run a close second. The earliest prosperity preachers were tent revivalists who used to get down into the crowd at the pinnacle of the service, rolling up their sleeves to lay their hands on the heads and limbs of trembling believers. And when they retired a tent—

because the audiences were either too large or too small—the enterprising preachers would cut these canvas cathedrals into little squares to mail to supporters, the fabric ostensibly saturated with healing power that people could hold in their hands. When Oral Roberts, famous televangelist and founder of the first charismatic university, wanted to help at-home audiences to believe, he used to raise his right hand to the camera so viewers could press their hands against the screen. The next best thing to skin on skin. They call these things "points of contact," the mediation of sacred power through objects. It is like God reaching out through something, bridging that last divide between divine and human, invisible and visible, spirit and flesh. These are points of contact, but they cannot be called sacraments because that would be too Catholic and it looks too Catholic already.

When I was in college, my gloriously hippie friends loved to make a huge deal about the fact that I was a Christian. I had not yet realized that Americans choose colleges based on their personalities. Everything I knew about college at that point I had picked up from the Saturday morning sitcom *Saved by the Bell,* and none of the characters had ever mentioned that delightfully liberal granola schools would not be filled with those who thought fondly of their years growing up in narrow-minded Christian towns. In fact, they would find you and your faith to be somewhat hilarious and, for a semester, submit your campus mailing address to prosperity preachers around the country. When you went to open your mailbox, it would be full of spiritual handkerchiefs to place on an afflicted body part, green oil to rub on your forehead, fake gold coins to tuck into your shoes, or any number of things to put under your pillow. The prosperity gospel is a faith meant to be touched and held.

I start to surround myself with *things*. Toban builds a little shelf to go beside the bed so that I can reach for books as I lie there. There are a few rows of practical items to make me feel useful—bottled water, light hand weights, and a stack of the latest American religious-history titles. Everything else is a friend. Two icons—one the looming figure of Archangel Michael and the other of St. Peregrine, an Italian friar and the patron saint of cancer patients—shine, their cracked-gold painted faces gazing at me. An old frame shows two blurry teenagers grinning at the camera. It was my first photo with Toban, and we are jumping for some reason. A little wooden piano plays a delicate tune and holds old Canadian bills, tarnished necklaces, and polished rocks my grandfather once collected. And on a large black canvas, a hand-drawn sign quoting the heroine of my favorite television show reads: "It's so weird being my own role model." I surround myself with reminders, things I can touch, that remind me of a time when I was Kate, and she could get out of bed.

LYING IN MY BED, I am trying to recover from surgery, but I have lost the habit of sleep. All the worst things happen in the dark. When I was in the hospital, I learned that when doctors want to tell you something, they will tell you at 4:00 A.M., when they start rounds and you are sleeping, and if it's really bad, they will send the person with the shortest lab coat. Seniority works in white coats, from the longest (read: fanciest head doctor) to the shortest (read: the greenest and most anxious doctor in the universe). So when I first heard how long I had to live, I drew the short coat. Apparently in research hospitals, this is a teaching moment. Find the person having the worst moment of her or his life, and send the intern. But my short coat was from Canada, so all mercy was granted. He sat down, and of everything he said, all I remembered was "You have a thirty to fifty percent chance of survival." By their definition, *survival* meant two years of life. And everything in my mind blurred and slowed. All I could think of to say was "If you're going to say stuff like that to me, you'd better be holding my hand." *Hold my hand*, I kept thinking. *Don't give up on me just yet.*

Everything around me is nudging me toward giving up hope that I will make it through this year. I am in the cancer clinic for a quick checkup on my surgical stitches and the physician assistant walks in. She moves through the pleasantries with enough warmth to suggest that, at least on social occasions, she considers herself to be a nice person.

"How are you?" she asks, pressing on my stomach lacerations as I stifle a sharp intake of breath.

"It's hard," I say, pretending to read the posters on the wall to keep myself from choking up.

"Well," she says, getting up and tidying the supplies, "the sooner you get used to the idea of dying the better." I stare at her, but she is zooming around the room and out the door, on to the next unfortunate recipient of her care. I get up and make it out of the cancer clinic before I crumple in a heap on the wooden bench next to the front door.

Sometime later I will meet a woman with my same cancer and my same life—a husband and a toddler—and she will say the words I was feeling in that moment:

"Aren't I still standing here, holding this purse?"

"Aren't I still stopping by the store to pick up ingredients for dinner tonight?"

I'm still real, aren't I?

THERE WAS ONE POINT in the hospital right after my surgery when I was allowed to see Zach. In those two minutes he looked up at me, furious and crying, with his hands in the air. He never screams, but he screamed at me because I was too weak to pick him up. And all I thought was, *I can't leave you here. Alone.*

It is an easy lie that has wormed its way into my mind: *I am the center that must hold.* It is a thought I picked up so early on in my life that I can't bring myself to question it. It is something closer to a reflex. Life is unstable because it is life. But I am steady.

My mother-in-law likes to make art out of colored wires, and she made me something sweet to put by my bed. It is three dangling hearts hanging in a long chain. A pink heart. A blue heart. A silver heart. Me, Toban,

Zach. And when I saw it, I immediately believed it as a lie about our love. *Yes, this all hangs on me. And it will all fall apart.*

My friend Carolyn and I are driving home from an appointment at the hospital a few weeks later, and she points to the local school as we drive by.

"Is that where Zach will go?" she says. A normal question said in a normal voice to a woman who doesn't know what any of that means anymore.

"I don't know, honey. I don't know if Toban and Zach will keep living here if I'm gone. They'll probably be in Canada."

My mind has skipped ahead to a patch of land north and west of the first Mennonite settlements in Manitoba. Toban's grandfather and uncle have a beautiful farm there, where the dirt is dark and rich as deep as you can dig a grave. *Rich as deep as you can dig a grave.* It's one of those offhanded comments that Uncle Kurt makes when he talks about the land, his lightly inflected German accent twisting poetry into all the talk of grain and fixing the silo on one side of the property. Not far away is the buried history of this Mennonite settlement, an unassuming cluster of gravestones beside a ditch by an old highway. Every tour I have ever gotten of the area includes that graveyard, and the constant reminder that it sits where the wooden German schoolhouse was and the old Mennonite church *used* to be.

There is an accidental beauty to being buried in the graveyard by the ditch, wedged between the memories of two institutions. If you want to get a plot there, you just have to call Abe from the town of Winkler, and he will dig one out for $250 including maintenance. It's a steal. All I want to tell Carolyn is that I don't know where Zach will be, but that she will probably find me between the ditch and the cornfield. But I can't tell her that. My brain is bouncing back and forth between two worn tracks—one set of plans that assume I will die and another equally sure I will survive. I make preparations just in case. I choose a preacher for my eulogy during a long, quiet moment.

Surrender seems like such a Christian word, as if I were letting go and sinking into the arms of God. Presbyterians, who are known for their staunch belief that God is the benevolent dictator of all that is good, would weep for joy at anyone who described herself as "surrendered." From the Presbyterian point of view I am a passive vehicle of God's grace. Like the lamb in Sunday school artwork, I am an adorable woolly passenger on Jesus' shoulders.

To believers in the prosperity gospel, surrender sounds like defeat. They write books with titles like *Deal with It!* to remind readers that there is nothing so difficult that God cannot accomplish it, and that you, sir or ma'am, had better get cracking. There are no setbacks, just setups. There are no trials, just tests of character. Tragedies are simply opportunities to claim a bigger, better miracle.

I often wonder if the prosperity gospel's never-give-up spirit produces resilient believers. Does it make happier people? Do people find themselves emboldened, shielded from the trials of daily life by the promise that they are more than conquerors? I can't tell. All I know is that a cheerful person can look a lot like someone with total mastery over everything that would weigh a lesser person down.

At the hospital, I can always spot prosperity believers by their desk space, because there will inevitably be Post-its taped around their monitors with little positive sayings ("You can't change the past, but you can change the future!") or scripture ("I can do all things through Christ who strengthens me!"). The nurses are harder to identify but come out like preachers if I happen to say anything negative.

"As they say, you got to name it and claim it," said

one nurse as she was drawing blood. "I just know that everything is going to work out!"

Control is a drug, and we are all hooked, whether or not we believe in the prosperity gospel's assurance that we can master the future with our words and attitudes. I can barely admit to myself that I have almost no choice but to surrender, but neither can those around me. I can hear it in my sister-in-law's voice as she tells me to keep fighting. I can see it in my academic friends, who do what researchers do and google the hell out of my problem. "When did the symptoms start?" they ask. "Is this hereditary?" Buried in all their concern is the unspoken question: Do I have any control?

A friend of a friend stops by with heaps and heaps of kale and flies around the kitchen with instructions about how to harness its healing properties. She is trying her best, I can see that, but I am slumped against the counter, half-listening in a fog of pain medication. Friends keep sending me recipes for green drinks and quinoa salads, and others ship herbal supplements straight to my house. *Just try, just try,* they are saying. *You can eat your way out of this.*

Toban and I get into a stupid fight when he finds me eating a huge, puffy Rice Krispies Treat. Don't I know that sugar causes cancer? He doesn't even believe that food has caused my particular cancer, but all this talk of nutrition has infected him with a poisonous hope. Maybe I can be the cure.

Infertility and disability should have taught me how to surrender, taught me how little I can control the conditions of my own happiness. Instead, that helplessness has only thickened my resolve to salvage what I can from the wreckage. If the physiotherapist says "One lap," I do two. When the doctor says, "You'll be out in four days," I push for three. I would like to blame it on some charming quirk—"I'm plucky!"—but it's more than that. I don't know how to stop. When I was little, my dad would read stories from Greek mythology, and I loved one most of all—that prideful king Sisyphus, who was doomed to roll a boulder up an impossibly steep hill only to have it roll down again. He would discover for all eternity that not every burden can be shouldered. *Yes,* I would think, learning nothing. *But at least he kept trying.*

My two best friends from Canada come with me for my first chemotherapy treatment and, like only best friends can, immediately invent nicknames for everyone we meet. There is Chipper Chad and Needle Nancy, but after a grim presentation by one of the nurses, Exaggerator Eve is born for her chilling words: "I've noticed that when people in chemotherapy get tired and take a nap, they never . . . get . . . up."

If I never nap. If I never complain. If I stifle my sharp intake of breath when I feel the pain. If I hide the reality, then maybe I'm not sick. So I continue to work full days. I get up at 6:30 A.M. every day—no matter what—so I won't miss a moment with my son. When I stop taking the medication that minimizes the numb feeling in my hands and feet, because I want to feel every shred of what is happening to me, my friends practically stage an intervention. When will I realize that surrender is not weakness?

St. Teresa of Avila once said: "We can only learn to know ourselves and do what we can—namely, surrender our will and fulfill God's will in us." For Christians not of the prosperity persuasion, surrender is a virtue; the writings of the saints are full of commands to "let go" and to submit yourself to what seems to be the will of the Almighty. All of American culture and pop psychology scream against that. Never give up on your dreams! Just keep knocking, that door is about to open! Think positively! Self-improvement guaranteed!! The entire motivational-speaking industry rests on the assumption that you can have what you want, you can be what you want. Just do it.

When prosperity believers live out their daily struggles with smiles on their faces, sometimes I want to applaud. They confront the impossible and joyfully insist that God make a way. They obediently put miracle oil on their failing bodies. They give large offerings to the church and expect great things. They stubbornly get out of their hospital beds and declare themselves healed, and every now and then, it works.

They are addicted to self-rule, and so am I.

CHAPTER 6

Christmas Cheer

THE LONG DAWN OF ADVENT WILL SOON BEGIN, and now we are all learning to wait. Christmas is coming and the baby Jesus will be born, but for now we must sit in the darkness.

I come from a Christmas home. I'm sure other people will say that they are Christmas enthusiasts, but—I say this with all sincerity—they are deceived. When I was growing up, we ate, breathed, and slept December 25. If there was a song to sing, it was a Christmas carol. If there was an inflatable member of the nativity scene that could be added to our front yard, it was waving in the wind. And if there was a pause on a long car ride on a hot July afternoon, it was because my dad was trying to come up with another way to ask: "Who is your favorite wise man?" Years ago, my dad started writing Christmas trivia quizzes for parties, and these grew into a number of historical books about Santa Claus and Christmas controversies, as well as a global encyclopedia of the holiday; these cost him ten years and roughly six hundred Christmas ornaments bought for "academic reasons." There is nothing my family loves more than our white Canadian Christmases in our crappy bungalow surrounded by blow-up Christmas figures that belong outside a car dealership.

This year I need Christmas, but not Christmas as usual. I need a miracle somewhat smaller than God becoming a baby and somewhat bigger than the promises of the Duke doctor who keeps using the word *palliative*.

Then at one of our appointments Dr. Palliative mentions that there are a few variables that might change the course of my treatment. Ninety percent of people with advanced colon cancer will receive chemotherapy and get their limited chance at life beyond five years. But there are two other options: I might be among the 7 percent of people who have a disorder in which cancer cells multiply beyond control so quickly that there is no treatment at all. It is an automatic death sentence. Or I might be among the remaining 3 percent who have a variation on that disorder that opens them up to possible new treatments. They'll give me a call in a couple of weeks and let me know.

"So, I either *maybe* live, die almost immediately, or have some kind of magic cancer that gets special treatments?" I ask.

"Pretty much," he says.

"Okay," I say. They have already drawn blood, and now I just have to wait for the results. As it turns out, the results come back in a couple of days, but I am too preoccupied to check my voice mail like a normal person. I get the news a week later, sitting outside, wrapped in blankets, fiddling with my phone.

"Hi, this is a call from the cancer clinic. We got your results back. The doctor said to tell you that you have the magic cancer, and that you'd know what that meant." I freeze. And then I play it again. And then one more time. I start to yell.

"I have the magic cancer! I have the magic cancer!"

Toban comes running out of the house, and I sink into his arms, crying. We are both trying to smile with that weary look of people overwhelmed by the prospect of hope.

"I might have a chance," I manage to say between

sobs. "I might have a chance." He hugs me tightly, resting his chin on my head. And then he releases me to let me sing "Eye of the Tiger" and do a lot of punching the air, because it is in my nature to do so.

The magic cancer, as it turns out, is a complicated gene mismatch repair disorder that I only partially understand. It is my ticket into clinical trials testing drugs not yet on the market. There is a trial opening up in the next few weeks seven hours away in Atlanta, at Emory University, and Dr. Now-Not-Saying-Palliative has sent my files there to start the application process. Before I can find out whether I'll make it into the trial, however, I need to get my medical insurance to cover it.

About an hour after I hear the news I begin to work the phones, slowly making my way through all the customer service representatives in the Emory and Duke insurance systems. Each university has a chain of people accustomed to saying no or, as I am beginning to suspect, they are evil robots masquerading as humans programmed to decline your every reasonable request. I try everything. My premium insurance will not cover anything outside of the Duke hospital system. I'm too poor to pay for it myself, but I don't qualify for charity care because I am not American. No matter how I parse it, paying as I go until I can get new insurance in January, just two months away, will cost me upward of $100,000. I know because I have had them price out the treatment down to every needle and scan.

By midafternoon, there is no one left to call, and the trial is not going to consider me without promise of payment. Either I have to come up with an impossible sum of money in the next few weeks or I will never get into the trial, and all my hopes built on magic cancer disappear into the ether. I slam down the phone at the end of the last call, blood boiling. I turn toward my parents. They have been staying with me since the surgery, trying to entertain Zach, keep the refrigerator full, and take me to my hospital visits.

"Don't worry," says my dad, putting down his book. "Your mother and I have $140,000 in liquid assets." I will only find out later that my family have all appraised their homes and savings plans—every last one of them—to see what they can cobble together to save my life. My best shot at survival will bankrupt my family. But my father keeps that impassive face and neutral voice that he always uses when everything is splitting at the seams. He has put his retirement and savings on the table to wager on a chance, any chance, for his daughter. But all I can see is cancer turning everyone upside down and shaking the pennies out of their pockets. Cancer wants to take it all.

"*I am not a normal person!*" I yell. It's a non sequitur. I don't know what it means, but I flush with rage and embarrassment when I realize that I'm shouting at the man who has spent most of his life working jobs beneath him to pay for my school, to buy my books, and to get me those juice boxes I like. I storm out of the house.

I pace through the backyard in the cooling air, weighing the math. I can't pay for this myself. Nothing plus nothing keeps equaling nothing.

I sit down on a bench and curl my knees into my chest. I have a terrible premonition that at the end of this once every stone is upturned and every drug tried—my family will have nothing left. I feel like an anvil dropped, crushing everything on its way down. I know it like I know the weight of my son's sleeping body in my arms. I will be the reason for the tall paper stacks of bills on the desk in the study, the second mortgage on my parents' aging home, the slope of their backs as they walk a little more heavily. They will carry my death in their checkbooks, vacations deferred, sleepless nights, and the silence of Sunday morning prayers when there is no daughter left to pray for. I am the death of their daughter. I am the death of his wife. I am the end of his mother. I am the life interrupted. Amen.

THIS WILL BE MY first Christmas away from Canada, away from my church on the one night when all the wanderers who no longer attend return to hug one another and sing carols like only Mennonites can, in growly German and perfect four-part harmony. I have always loved the darkness and the candles during "Silent Night." Mostly I love the feeling of homecoming I get when I see Liz, who designed my prom dress in a shiny lavender poly-satin, and Ferd, who quietly nailed the cross back together after my friend and I accidentally broke it in an ill-advised reenactment of the crucifixion on a youth group overnight. I never told my parents and, God bless him, neither did Ferd. I look forward to getting a fierce hug from Charlotte, my mom's best friend, and my old Sunday school teacher Carol, who helped me get into my sheep costume for the Christmas pageant year after year.

A couple of Christmases ago, I saw Carol over one of the pews and reached out to give her a hug, remembering only at the last second that she had recently been diagnosed with cancer. I couldn't figure out what to say when we pulled away and I found I was just staring into her smiling face, stammering something about how sorry I was. She looked back at me with such calm and said something I had never heard anyone say.

"I have known Christ in so many good times," she said, sincerely and directly. "And now I will know Him better in His sufferings."

She meant it. And I could not imagine a world in which I could mean it. It was Christmas, and I was busy with presents, coffee dates, and rushing between family gatherings. It was only partway through the service that I began to hope that that Christmas feeling would sink in as the night gathered and the music slowed. The angels were singing and the Wise Men were on their way and all the church was ready for Jesus to be born, but I hardly noticed. I wasn't asking God for anything in particular. Carol surely wanted healing and more years with her husband and an escape from the creeping death that is multiplying cells and the fading powers of chemotherapy drugs. And yet she prayed for more than to be saved. She prayed in the long night of Advent that her waiting would end with a better angle of vision on the baby born to die.

Toban encouraged me to put up the Christmas tree

in October, and we trimmed the house with toasted pinecones, bushy evergreen branches, and golden baubles. First thing in the morning, Zach loves to sprint from his room, his chubby arms pumping, to make sure he is there when I flick on the lights to the tree. He laughs maniacally every time, tossing his head back with an evil "Ha! Ha! Ha!" like Vincent Price. I taught him how to do that, and I have never regretted it. Then he pulls a thick blanket over to where I am sitting and tucks us both into it. He looks up at me and smiles broadly.

God, I don't want to just know you better. I want to save my family.

STILL SITTING ON THE outdoor bench with my phone, I shoot off an email to the only two professors I know with some connections to the hospital. I tell them that I've been turned down by insurance, and that I am at the end of what I can do. My mind is circling around the same obsessive thought: *I am ruining everything for everyone I love.* Both professors write back immediately with just a few words. "I'm on it." "Let me see what I can do."

The thing I love most about my friends is summed up

by their reaction to my ridiculous request. Later, one of them will tell me exactly what he had said to himself: "Thank God! Something I can do!" Their love has arms and legs and momentum. Their love has reach.

As it turns out, they will shake the bushes for me. They will email everyone they know and, after my useless efforts to get anyone to even talk to me, I watch with equally helpless shock as the emails start to pour in, emails from famous people with Wikipedia pages and their names on buildings. These two professors pull the right levers and know whom to ask; they have pleaded for me at every level of these institutions, and within twenty-four hours I have multiple assurances from what feels like the queen on down to the janitor that I will see only green lights from now on. My family will be spared; I might be saved. I have squeezed through the cracks in the system and found my way back into the sun even though, really, I have done nothing at all. It has all been done for me.

The prosperity gospel has a word for that feeling that God is on your side. It's called "favor" in a very particular sense. When a man stands up in a church service to testify that his boss gave him the company car and free gas to go visit his ailing father, shouts of "Favor! Favor!" erupt from the congregation. When a woman tells a friend that her bid for a house she would like to buy has been accepted, despite heavy competition, her friend whoops with a cry of "Favor!" The wind is at your back. It's what insiders claim is the protection of God at every turn but outsiders might simply call luck. "I'm not a normal person," one of them might say.

With the insurance obstacles clearing, the clinical trial folks ask me to come down for a preliminary screening or, as I start to call it, my tryout. They want to take my blood, run some tests, and see if I qualify as a desirable candidate in their selective study. Now I am just worried that I might be disqualified because I am still bleeding from my surgery incisions. I am trying to keep that to myself, but at one point even I have to admit I am not doing terribly well, and Toban drives me to the emergency room late at night. A kindly doctor lets me skip the hours-long wait and leads us into what amounts to a spare closet with a flickering fluorescent light, a single chair, and no supplies. He is doing me a favor, seeing me with no notice, and has to scrounge for what he needs before he asks me to lift my shirt and show him what we are dealing with. It's gross because it is infected, and we all know it, but I am determined to make small talk to show my appreciation for his efforts and not to make a peep about the treatment. The treatment, as it turns out, hurts so much that it makes my eyes water. It looks a lot like someone trying to squeeze wine out of grapes by hand and sounds a lot like MASH MASH MASH MASH MASH, which makes Toban gag as I am trying to look around pleasantly and comment on the state of world news. When the doctor steps back, it looks like a murder scene. But for some reason, the whole thing is so funny to me that, once Toban stops retching into his cupped hands, I resolve to stow it away in the memory bank as "Fun in Retrospect."

My nerves are on edge on the morning of my departure. I wake up and pack the wounds as quietly as possible before I go downstairs to lift my tiny human out of his crib. I grind the coffee beans while Zach and I yell at the top of our lungs to match the pitch of the grinder. We do it every day, and I'd like to think we're getting better at it. I hate to leave him for these few days of testing, as everything still feels too precious and this love makes me clingy and tender. But my dad and I pack our things and say our goodbyes, promising that we will stop at every oversize landmark and text everyone with any bit of news.

Cancer clinics try to be places of encouragement, and for that we can offer them a slow hand clap. But mostly they are encounters with death set to the tune of a young volunteer on the lobby's baby grand piano and the muffled sounds of someone yelling, *"Mr. Smith! It's your turn for blood work!"* When I heard a harp player in the foyer, I immediately turned to my dad and said: "Is it really *that* bad?"

Pale and puffy, the patients lean their heads on the hard edges of the seats beside them or sink onto the bony shoulders of their companions. Everyone looks up when a name is called, momentarily revived. There are wheelchairs everywhere and bald, wrinkled women in bright kerchiefs and someone coughing blood beside a mural that reads: LAUGHTER IS THE BEST MEDICINE! Lord, I hope not.

Everyone I meet is kind and efficient, and I try to accept what is happening like it's my first day of work. The bruising needle marks will go away, I tell myself, and the scan was not so bad because I made Sam, the technician, tell me his life story. "Start at the beginning," I said as he injected the dye. "Leave nothing out." He took that so seriously that by the time I had left the room, he had just been born.

Then there is nothing left to do. The doctors will review the charts and let me know if I qualify. As we walk past the sign for the cancer clinic, I stop my dad and hand him my phone.

"Take a picture, Dad. When I get in the trial, people are going to want to see me in this moment."

I raise my clasped hands in the air in a gesture of salute and plaster a huge smile on my face. It is getting colder out, even in Atlanta, and it occurs to me that it is autumn and I might not get another summer. I grit my teeth into a bigger smile. He takes a few pictures, and we walk to the car quietly before my dad breaks the silence to ask me something I love about Christmas. But I can already feel the shape of a question looming in my mind: *Who takes a picture of something she is begging God for?*

In the darkness of the car ride home to my family and the baby asleep in his bed, I can't help but think about the person in the photo, who pretended she wasn't on the edge of dying. Her cheerfulness. Her sunny-side-up Facebook posts brimming with positivity and gently ironic updates. Is that really me?

"*I am not a normal person!*" I had shouted, to myself and to my father and to God. Even though I did not solve my own insurance debacle or create the biology to have "magic cancer," I have still, somehow, clung to the idea that I am able to save myself. To my friends and family, I sugarcoat the truth with spiritual-sounding assurances and good cheer.

There is an inchoate sadness in the pit of my stomach, hard to express. I try to focus on the more superficial things that are out of my control. I feel sick when I look at the crisscrossing scars on my stomach. I hate running my fingers through my hair because I can feel the light tearing of my scalp and see the little tufts of hair that come off in my hands. I walk past a gym and watch the women work out as if I'm an alien who crash-landed on a planet of the carefree and healthy. I know I am going to be getting chemotherapy no matter what, but when it was announced that I would be wearing a giant sack filled with chemotherapy fluid in a bag around my waist, attached to a giant needle that goes into the port beside my heart, I am just *thrilled* to be bringing fanny packs back into style. And since I always need to wear my backpack to carry my medical equipment, I am essentially wearing bags on bags on bags.

"Some women BeDazzle it," says an older nurse, helpfully.

"Yes, this certainly needs a heck of a lot more rhinestones," I say, looking it over. "Something that says 'BLESSED!' . . . or something."

"Or something," says the nurse, and we silently agreed that it is hideous in all its forms.

When I started chemotherapy, I tried to hide all its varieties of ugliness. I posted pretty self-portraits on Facebook and named my portable chemo pack Jimmy after I saw former president Jimmy Carter at the cancer center twice and announced to everyone that we would develop a lifelong friendship. Everyone knew that Kate had cancer and that for her it was basically a special pass to understand the life and times of Jimmy Carter. People had something to ask about and to point to that was sweet and funny. No one had to lead with "Soooo . . . you have cancer." Instead, it was always "So, how's Jimmy?" I couldn't stand that people might see through me—that they might know I was only another tired cancer patient with a creeping sense of hopelessness and the glorious delusion that sheer willpower would make the difference.

In the storefront prosperity church I studied for years, the congregation managed the spectacle of pain with ceaseless positivity. A singer's congested voice can't hit the high notes, and other women begin to shout encouragement. A woman slumps into her seat, and the people around her start to sing about how far she's come, to the tune of "Look What the Lord Has Done." An elder once preached his Sunday school message on this determined joy by imitating a limping man still shouting with delight that he was already healed. He could limp his way, by utter determination, into God's favor.

When I think about where sheer grit has gotten me, I can't help but remember standing in the parking lot outside my pregnancy education class, seven months pregnant, having a panic attack. Somehow the reality of my already massive baby making a massive exit sent me completely over the edge, and I ran out of the room, trying not to lose it in front of a gaggle of overly fashionable soon-to-be moms. But then Toban gave me the greatest speech ever given, which, looking back, I realize sounded a lot like the battle cry from Shakespeare's *Henry V* ("We few! We happy few!") but ended with *"Look at them!"* (He pointed dramatically through the window at the women taking the class.) "Do any of *them* look like they can crank out an enormous baby? *Those* little wimps? One lady just asked for filtered water, Kate. *Filtered water!*" I started to laugh, which meant I had started to breathe again. "You are going to go. back. in. there. and learn how to *have. this. baby*!" And then we marched back in there with Toban quietly percussing the theme song to *Chariots of Fire*.

I have been all kinds of cheery. But positivity has become a burden. And it's a burden I assumed when I decided that, in the darkness of Advent, I would save myself.

At the end of the week I get a phone call from Emory saying that I have qualified for the study. My parents shout and dance, and Toban picks Zach up and twirls him around like a carousel horse.

"See?" I say to my dad. "I'm not a normal person."

"No," he says softly, reaching out to pull me to him. "You're a superhero. But I wish you didn't have to be."

CHAPTER 7

Certainty

THE TREATMENT AT EMORY BEGINS AT THE END of October. I am tired most of the time, but I feel driven to catalog everything and wring every bit of time for all it's worth. I start to write. In bed, in chemo chairs, in waiting rooms, I try to say something about dying in a world where everything happens for a reason. Whenever there is a clarifying moment of grief, I jot it down. And then, in a flurry, I shoot it off to *The New York Times,* not thinking too much about whether it's any good, but sending it because I have been infected by the urgency of death. Then an editor there sees it, and puts it on the front page of the Sunday Review. Millions of people read it. Thousands share it and start writing to

me. And most begin with the same words. "I'm afraid."
Me too, me too.

"I'm afraid of the loss of my parents," writes a young
man. "I know I will lose them someday soon, and I
can't bear the thought." "I'm afraid for my son," says a
father from Arkansas. "He has been diagnosed with a
brain tumor at forty-four, which would have been dev-
astating enough if he had not already lost his identical
twin brother to the same disease a few years ago."
These letters sing with unspeakable love in the face of
the Great Separation. *Don't go, don't go, you anchor
my life.*

It feels as though the world has been cracked open,
and it bleeds and bleeds. Hundreds of emails, letters,
pictures, and videos pour into my in-box and campus
mailbox. A mother writes about her son dying young of
lung cancer. He never smoked. A nurse has survived ten
years past her Stage IV cancer diagnosis, but her healthy
husband suddenly dies one day from an undetected
brain bleed. A middle-aged woman has buried her son
after watching bill collectors hunt him, and hospitals,
whose treatments would have saved his life, reject him.
A check from Medicaid arrives in the mail nine days
after his death.

Strangers pour out their fury at every stage of their

own grief. Depression settles on the pages like a fog. A young man writes: "I guess I was hoping that God would make something of this. But it has come to nothing." The void is deep and bottomless. And it is an unmerciful fact that some people have the right to look into my eyes and say, "You're lucky." A young woman gently explains to me that cancer had stolen her fertility only months before she met the love of her life. If ever she shakes the disease, even for a little, she will try to adopt. "Hold your son close, you're so fortunate to have him." There is plenty of denial, and plenty of the deals people attempt to broker with God. "I am an atheist, but I put it aside, and I begged God to take the cancer away from my son and to put it into me." I read that letter to my father, who is sitting in an overstuffed leather chair in my living room holding his Kindle two inches from his glasses.

"Oh, I've prayed that a hundred times. 'Please, God, why not just take me?'" he says a little wistfully. I scoot over beside him and rest my head on his knee.

"Dad, that is about the kindest, saddest thing I've ever heard." There is a gentle silence between us as I imagine that we are both thinking about how much we love each other before my dad begins to speak.

"But then I remember that God didn't spare Mozart

at your age . . . so . . ." He is making a gesture that suggests he is weighing a heavy object in each hand. "So, you know." I start to laugh.

"What did he die of?"

"The plague, I think."

"Oh, geez."

"Yeah. And God loves you at least as much as Mozart."

"Let's go back to loving each other in silence."

A hilarious number of letters basically start with "You think *you* have it bad?! Listen to *this*!" followed by a litany of complaints. The weirdest part is not simply that, yes, I do feel Stage IV cancer is a bit rough, but that these are letters written by people at the ends of long lives. A seventy-three-year-old woman named Trudy writes me to say that cancer can't be nearly as terrible as learning she was adopted. *Um, okay, can't they both be bad?* The pain of the world is being calculated, and according to some, compassion can be doled out only by the teaspoon.

I can't fully understand the people who write to say that, sorry, their lives have been grand. I receive long accounts of how deeply satisfied some people are with their many, many achievements. "Younger by the day!" boasts an elderly pastor.

But many people write to me like family. "As a father, I am truly sorry." "I'm a mother and I wish I could give you a hug right now." They want to comfort me, but their experiences tell them that life is never fair. "I want you to know how much I'm praying for you and grateful for your faith. I'm sorry that we must say, like Job, 'Though He slay me, yet will I trust in Him.'" *Yes, yes, yes. Yet will I trust in Him. I don't know what the word "trust" means anymore, except there are moments when I realize that it feels a lot like love.*

I'VE BEEN IN TREATMENT for five months, and now it is Palm Sunday. When we get to church, the children's Sunday school is closed, so we are faced with the terror of having a two-year-old in the main Sunday service. The sanctuary is swimming with children. They spin in circles, they climb on top of each other, but mostly they hit each other with palm fronds. In Christian art, a palm frond is a symbol of martyrdom, a little reminder to the viewer that this saint has earned his or her status in blood. But at every Palm Sunday service, the only whiff of martyrdom is the sense that every child is about three seconds from getting a palm frond in the eyeball.

A tired volunteer still manages a smile and hands one to my two-year-old, who is delighted.

Suddenly, the organ music swells and the doors fly open, and the procession has begun. It is, as all children's programming is, completely absurd and wonderful. Some children refuse to move past the pews that hold their parents. Others sprint ahead. Three begin to cry. But most are trying to hit their brothers in the eye. Zach is utterly still as he takes in the view. I know what he is seeing. His small world has not yet included vaulted ceilings and warm wooden beams and window after window of colored glass. One of his arms is wrapped around my neck, and the other is pointing everywhere as his wide blue eyes scan the room. We march up to the front of the sanctuary. Everyone is smiling broadly as they stomp around the room. So taken are we by the spectacle of radiant youth that nobody is looking at the hymnal, and the space fills with loud, unself-conscious singing.

I catch Toban's eye as I hold Zach like a prize lamb, and I can tell he is trying not to cry. We are thinking the same thing: *Is this one of those moments? The kind that he will have to look back on alone?* I hold Zach up a little higher so he can wave his frond in the air, and I try to smile as a few tears trickle down my cheeks. I know where Palm Sunday falls in the story of our God. Jesus is on a donkey trudging into Jerusalem, people waving their arms in the air, tattered coats thrown down before the One who marches toward His death. It is a celebration. It is a funeral procession. Holding Zach in my arms, fifteen days from my next scan, I wish I knew the difference.

MY IN-BOX IS FULL of strangers giving reasons. People offer them to me like wildflowers they picked along the way. A few people want me to cultivate spiritual acceptance. "We have had many millions of births and deaths in different life-forms," explains a Hindu woman gently. "Don't worry, this life shall pass and your soul will move forward to its next step." The world is a place of suffering, they write, a garden full of weeds that we tend as best we can.

But most everyone I meet is dying to make me certain. They want me to know, without a doubt, that there is a hidden logic to this seeming chaos. Even when I was still in the hospital, a neighbor came to the door and told my husband that everything happens for a reason.

"I'd love to hear it," he replied.

"Pardon?" she said, startled.

"The reason my wife is dying," he said in that sweet and sour way he has, effectively ending the conversation as the neighbor stammered something and handed him a casserole.

Christians want me to reassure them that my cancer is all part of a plan. A few letters even suggest that God's plan was that I get cancer so I could help people by writing the *New York Times* article. There is a circular logic to these attempts to explain the course of any life. If you inspire people while dying, the plan for your life was that you would become an example to others. If you don't and you die kicking and screaming, the plan was that you discover some important divine lessons. Either way, learn to accept God's plan.

It is at moments like this—when I feel everyone's eyes on me, watching my progress and my attitude for signs of the gospel—that I am gripped with fear. If I hear the news—if the scan comes back and the oncologist says that my days won't be renewed—will I scream or sit quietly? Will I feel peace or will I beat the ground? *God, will you make a fool of me?*

What if everything is random? A woman who has left the faith for science writes: "I find it comforting to believe the universe is random, because then the God I believe in is no longer cruel." This is a painful conclusion for so many who comb through the details of their tragedies and find no evidence that God was ever there. The world, it seems, is also filled with fathers and mothers begging for their children's lives and hearing nothing but silence. And, ever after, every church service that sings that God is good rattles like tin in their ears. There can be only one reasonable conclusion, says a father whose children have all been cut down by disease: no one is listening.

The spring is trying to make everything new, but my world feels increasingly dark. The chemotherapy drugs are cranked up so high that my feet are tender. I've been plagued with lockjaw and cold hypersensitivity, so that every time I touch anything cool it feels like I am being zapped with electricity. I am so forgetful about this that Toban hangs a sign on the freezer with a picture of MC Hammer that reads: GIRL, U CAN'T TOUCH THIS. It is increasingly hard to remember that these side effects are not the same as dying. My toenail came off in my sock yesterday, and my first thought was that it would spook people if I told them. I keep my voice firm and strong, but I feel as fragile as glass.

"Why are you dying?" writes a man from Idaho.

"Some people might think it's cruel for God to let you die so young. But the answer is simple and crystal clear. God is a just God to let you die. This is the consequence for your sin." I receive that little word of encouragement while I sit in a hospital waiting room, watching a woman cough flecks of red, red blood onto her white sweater. She sinks back into her chair. We are all the choir of the damned.

MY FRIEND JODY IS sitting in my office, her head in her hands. Her mom is dying of a brain tumor and it is exhausting. Dying is exhausting.

"But I'm sure you are feeling so very fortunate for all the shared time you had together," I say. She looks up abruptly and then immediately catches my mood.

"Yes, so very fortunate," she replies with a tone that suggests homicide is a viable response to people who say these kinds of things. "People keep telling me how fortunate I am."

I let the sarcasm drop from my voice and put my hand on her shoulder.

"I'm sorry, hon. I wish I never had to hear the words 'at least' again. At least I'm at a top-rated medical facility. At least I'm trying the new drug. Yesterday I found out that my insurance got screwed up and they sent my bill to debt collectors. *Debt collectors*." We look at each other with the shared weariness of people tired at the oars. "So guess what someone said?"

"No," she says.

"*Yes!* They said: 'At least you have the financial and intellectual resources to deal with it.'"

She gives a low whistle.

"Why is everyone trying to teach us a lesson?" she asks, and we both feel tired just thinking about it.

THESE ARE THE THREE life lessons people try to teach me that, frankly, sometimes feel worse than cancer itself. The first is that I shouldn't be so upset, because the significance of death is relative. I like to call the people with that message the Minimizers. Some people do it spiritually by reminding me that, cosmically, death isn't the ultimate end. "It doesn't matter, in the End, whether we are here or 'there.' It's all the same," writes a woman in the prime of her youth. She includes a lot of praying hand emoticons. A lot of Christians like to remind me that heaven is my true home, which makes me want to ask them if they would like to go home first. Maybe now? And atheists can be equally trite by demanding that I immediately give up any search for meaning. Someone else writes that my faith is holding me hostage to an inscrutable God. I should let go of this guesswork—these ridiculous theological reasons—and realize that we are living in an uncaring and neutral universe. But the message is the same: stop complaining and accept the world as it is.

"We can't always get what we want," writes one woman, as if chiding me for asking for dessert. It reminds me of the many times in studying the prosperity gospel that I was chided for complaining. The moratorium on negative speech is so thoroughgoing that I only really saw one giant display of insubordination. I was on a trip to a particularly blingy megachurch that insisted on spray-painting everything in gold. The church had set up a large wooden cross on the grounds so that believers could write prayer requests and nail them, metaphorically and literally, to the cross. When I went to tack my prayer up, I saw that someone had already put a note front and center: "I pray that this church would spend more money on employee compensation and less money on golden lions."

The second lesson comes from the Teachers, who focus on how this experience is supposed to be an education in mind, body, and spirit. "I suppose that this is the ultimate test of faith for you," one man muses, hoping that I will have the good sense to accept God's will. "Anyway," he says at the close of the letter, "I'll pray for your remission, and if you die that your suffering is minimal." *Thanks, Joe from Indiana.* Sometimes I want every know-it-all to send me a note when *they* face the grisly specter of death, and I'll send them a cat poster that says HANG IN THERE!

"I hope you have a 'Job' experience," writes one man bluntly, and I can't think of anything worse to wish on someone. God allowed Satan to rob Job of everything, including his children's lives. *Do I need to lose something more to learn God's character?* In these moments, I love the people who write to me with their simple, unvarnished conclusions. "Um . . . yeah," writes a young man after describing how diseases are cutting down his family one by one. "The question of 'What the f**k?' is pretty much on target every day."

The hardest lessons come from the Solutions People, who are already a little disappointed that I am not saving myself. "Keep smiling! Your attitude determines your destiny!" says Jane from Idaho, and I am immediately worn out by the tyranny of prescriptive joy.

Because of my background in the prosperity gospel, I receive hundreds of letters from those inside the movement. These are people who, crushed by the weight of solution-focused theology, have been unable to grieve. A Nigerian woman sits through weekly meetings at her job encouraging her to "talk faith-talk," but she wants to acknowledge that, outside her office window, the bodies of abandoned babies are being collected and hauled away in black refuse bags. A bitter seed has been planted in a young father who must take his brain-dead child off life support while his extended family, steeped in prosperity theology, rails against him for his inability to prevent his child's death. I receive so many stories like this, the laments of bereaved parents who are asked to keep a smile on their faces.

There is a trite cruelty in the logic of the perfectly certain. Those letter writers are not simply trying to give me something. They are also, always, tallying up the sum of my life, sometimes for clues, sometimes for answers, always to pronounce a verdict. But I am not on trial.

THE LETTERS THAT REALLY speak to me don't talk about why we die, they talk about *who* was there. When you were afraid that the end had come, were you alone?

A man writes to me about being taken hostage with

his family and watching helplessly as the intruders pressed guns against his children's noses while his wife and daughter were threatened with rape. But God was there and he can't explain it. He can't explain who loosened the ropes and let him escape with his family unharmed. And he will never understand why he survived when his neighbor was found outside hanging by a rope the next morning. He doesn't rationalize why some people are rescued and others are hanged and doubts there is a way that God "redeems" situations by extracting good from them. But he knows God was there because he felt peace, indescribable peace, and it changed him forever. He ends the letter with a shrug: "I have no idea how this works, but I wish this for you as you move forward."

His description matches something I read in the newspaper the other day that summarized the findings of the Near Death Experience Research Foundation, and, yes, there is such a thing. Thousands of people were interviewed about their brushes with death in every kind of situation—being in a car accident, giving birth, attempting suicide, et cetera—and many described the same odd thing: love. I'm sure I would have ignored the article if it had not reminded me of something that happened to me, something that I felt uncomfortable telling anyone. It seemed too odd and too simplistic to say what I knew to be true—that when I was sure I was going to die, I didn't feel angry. I felt loved.

In those first few days after my diagnosis, when I was in the hospital, I couldn't see my son, I couldn't get out of bed, and I couldn't say for certain that I would survive the year. But I felt as though I'd uncovered something like a secret about faith. Even in lucid moments, I found my feelings so difficult to explain. I kept saying the same thing: "I don't want to go back. I don't want to go back."

At a time when I should have felt abandoned by God, I was not reduced to ashes. I felt like I was floating, floating on the love and prayers of all those who hummed around me like worker bees, bringing notes and flowers and warm socks and quilts embroidered with words of encouragement. They came in like priests and mirrored back to me the face of Jesus.

When they sat beside me, my hand in their hands, my own suffering began to feel like it had revealed to me the suffering of others, a world of those who, like me, are stumbling in the debris of dreams they thought they were entitled to and plans they didn't realize they had made.

That feeling stayed with me for months. In fact, I had grown so accustomed to that floating feeling that I started to panic at the prospect of losing it. So I began to ask friends, theologians, historians, pastors I knew, and nuns I liked, *What am I going to do when it's gone?* And they knew exactly what I meant because they had either felt it themselves or read about it in great works of Christian theology. St. Augustine called it "the sweetness." Thomas Aquinas called it something mystical like "the prophetic light." But all said yes, it will go. The feelings will go. The sense of God's presence will go. There will be no lasting proof that God exists. There will be no formula for how to get it back.

But they offered me this small bit of certainty, and I clung to it. When the feelings recede like the tides, they said, they will leave an imprint. I would somehow be marked by the presence of an unbidden God.

It is not proof of anything. And it is nothing to boast about. It was simply a gift. I can't reply to the thousands of emails with my own Five-Step Plan to Divine Health or series of powerful formulas, which guarantee results. I suppose I am like the man who wrote to me to say he had seen a friend swinging from a tree and felt the presence of God in the same long, dark night. *Yes. That is the God I believe in.*

—

I CAN'T RECONCILE THE way that the world is jolted by events that are wonderful and terrible, the gorgeous and the tragic. Except I am beginning to believe that these opposites do not cancel each other out. I see a middle-aged woman in the waiting room of the cancer clinic, her arms wrapped around the frail frame of her son. She squeezes him tightly, oblivious to the way he looks down at her sheepishly. He laughs after a minute, a hostage to her impervious love. Joy persists somehow and I soak it in. The horror of cancer has made everything seem like it is painted in bright colors. I think the same thoughts again and again: Life is so beautiful. Life is so hard.

THE FLOW OF LETTERS has slowed, but I still get at least one every day. Today I received a book in my campus mailbox about how to guarantee that I will communicate with my loved ones from heaven, and a handwritten card about scriptures I could repeat aloud to become a better conduit of God's power. A pastor from a prosperity church has mailed me a large manila folder containing an enormous banner that reads: SEEK

YE FIRST THE KINGDOM OF GOD AND ALL THESE THINGS SHALL BE ADDED UNTO YOU. I can't help but think it's a little passive-aggressive, but I appreciate the gesture. Sort of. He is asking me to employ a series of proven techniques that could help me reclaim my own health, if I would only try.

This is the problem, I suppose, with formulas. They are generic. But there is nothing generic about a human life. When I was little, to get to my bus stop, I had to cross a field that had so much snow my parents fitted me with ski pants and knee-high thermal boots that were toasty to forty degrees below zero. I am excellent in the stern of a canoe, but I never got the hang of riding a bike with no hands. I have seen the northern lights because my parents always woke up the whole house when the night sky was painted with color. I love the smell of clover and chamomile because my sister and I used to pick both on the way home from swimming lessons. I spent weeks of my childhood riding around on my bike saving drowning worms after a heavy rain. My hair is my favorite feature even though it's too heavy for most ponytails, and I still can't parallel park. There is no life *in general*. Each day has been a collection of trivial details—little intimacies and jokes and screw-ups and realizations. My problems can't be solved by those

formulas—those clichés—when my life was never generic to begin with. God may be universal, but I am
not. I am Toban's wife and Zach's mom and Karen and
Gerry's daughter. I am here now, bolted in time and
place, to the busy sounds of a blond boy in dinosaur
pajamas crashing into every piece of furniture.

"Who's my baby?" I ask him.

Zach is running long loops around the room and
stopping at every ledge to run his car along it. He turns
to me.

"A boy?" he says hopefully.

"Yes," I say, scooping him into my arms. He tolerates
my tight hug for a few breaths and then squirms his way
out, laughing. "Yes." I say. "But not just any boy. You."

CHAPTER 8

Restoration

I HAVE TAKEN UP CURSING FOR LENT, THE FORTY-DAY stretch before Easter in which those who want to understand Jesus' sacrifice choose one of their own. They promise to abandon vices, take up new spiritual practices, or simply give up chocolate like every fourteen-year-old girl I knew at St. Mary's Academy, who combined their sympathy with Jesus at his grisly crucifixion with a spring break weight-loss program. As adults, most do-gooders I know give up alcohol or spend more time in prayer. I've started swearing.

And I mean it. I swear about cancer. I swear about dry croissants and coffee that cools too quickly. I swear about the budding ulcers in my mouth from intense chemotherapy. I swear about the refugee crisis in Europe. I swear before and after I receive test results even though I'm tremendously relieved that, so far, the tumors are still shrinking. I swear about Curious George whining to the Man in the Yellow Hat. I am relentless. Last week I cursed at my mother-in-law in what I imagine was the halfway mark of her complaining about her wrinkles and her droopy parts.

"I think aging is a fucking privilege," I say squarely.

There is a silence between us at the Starbucks where we are sitting, but then she begins to laugh loudly. She has a great laugh that always whoops up to a nice, satisfying sound of shock.

"Oh, well, *yes*. I suppose it is! Yes." She leans over the table and hugs me, and then she picks up where she left off because she has been my mom, too, since I was fourteen and I first met Toban. She has hummed along beside me during all the seasons of my life since, and it's not her fault that this season is beginning to spark something close to rage.

I read an article about how people in grief swear because they feel the English language has reached its limit in a time of inarticulate sorrow. Or at least that is what I tell people when I am casually dropping f-bombs over lunch as I explain the mysteries of Lent.

I have, rather childishly, told God that I will stop swearing at the end of Lent, but the truth is, I'm swearing *because* of Lent.

It started on Ash Wednesday. I had another set of scans, and Katherine, one of my very best friends, drove hours to Atlanta so we could wait together for the results. We found an Ash Wednesday service at a local Catholic church because I have always loudly proclaimed that Catholics, of all God's children, are wonderful at being sad. I have seen the mourning of Lent a million times, from Ash Wednesday to Holy Saturday: The sad kiss of an overturned cross at the front of a chapel, scraping their knees on the floor as they ignore the stares of strangers and friends. The shuffle past the inscriptions around the church marking the Stations of the Cross. When the priest dips his thumb in the black ash of burnt palm leaves, marking foreheads with the sign of the cross, he whispers the last part of Genesis 3:19:

> *Pulvis es, et in pulverem reverteris.*
> From dust you came,
> and to dust you will return.

It is so grim. There is no denying our finitude. It is plain and hard and true.

Unfortunately, Katherine and I stumble upon a thriving Catholic church for all the loveliest people, I'm sure, who want to hear the ways in which Lent is about making us a tiny bit better. The priest actually uses the phrase "tiny bit" as he describes how this might be possible. *Think about volunteering once or twice. Be nice to people at work. Don't forget that your gifts are special!* Then he doles out the ashes with all the cheer of Snow White sending her industrious dwarves off to the mines.

A few years ago I was in Houston, the megachurch capital of the country, interviewing prosperity leaders or representatives of some of the nation's largest churches. I had not meant to arrive there in the busy Holy Week, but I found myself on Good Friday with nothing to do but hope that people might be free to talk on the darkest day of the Christian year. Seeing nothing on the church websites, I spent the afternoon calling around to see which service I could attend. It was *awkward*. Most were not holding services, but I was encouraged to come back on Sunday, when Jesus was risen. One lady who answered the phone baldly told me that she had no idea what I was talking about when I said "Good Friday." Lakewood Church, Joel and Victoria Osteen's megachurch, was the only one with a Good

Friday service, and I was, pen and paper in hand, going to be there.

Lakewood Church holds services in the former Compaq Center arena, where the Houston Rockets used to play, and attendees have to make their way from the parking deck, up endless escalators, and around the cavernous main stage to their seats like any devoted fans. An army of cheerful volunteers are scattered throughout the seemingly endless space to facilitate your transition from Houston freeway exiter to worshipful participant, except, on this day, business as usual seemed odd.

"Happy Good Friday!" yelled the parking attendant, flashing his glowing traffic wand.

"Happy Good Friday!" chirped the woman stationed at the bottom of the escalator.

By the umpteenth greeting, "Happy Good Friday!" seemed like the order of the day. This was, I suspected, going to be the hap-happiest Good Friday service I had ever attended.

To the Osteens' credit, Jesus stayed dead for about three songs in the opening worship set. As the worship band played and a white mist rose to the ceiling in puffy clouds of Holy Spirit smoke, the tone stayed appropriately serious. I won't say it was somber, but it might qualify as, at least, solemn. Each song undergirded the sense that the death of Jesus was meant to solve the problem of our sin, and that God was, indeed, *very* good. Then Victoria Osteen appeared from backstage, her stiletto heels clicking as she entered with a toothy smile.

"Isn't it great we serve a risen Lord!" she asked rhetorically.

On a day and at an hour during which, historically, Christians refuse to speak the word *Alleluia* ("Christ is risen") in song or prayer, Victoria loudly skipped the moment in the tradition where Jesus is conspicuously absent. He died that day. And his disciples were, in their despair, quite convinced that he was never coming back.

The English language is already a bit confused in calling the day "good" while other languages settled on Holy Friday or Great Friday or, even better, Black Friday. We call it something that might have once been "God's Day" and mull over the paradox that made it so. We have fallen in love with a God who abandons His child to die, a son who begs for His own life but, seeing it cannot be helped, gives Himself over to His murderers. He seemed like He would save them all, but on this day He just hangs there off the wood He has been nailed to.

But Victoria was right, in a way. There was nothing particularly Good Fridayish about the fog pouring in through the deep blue ceiling. There was nothing especially sad about the actual live lamb that trotted onstage during the sermon, softly bleating as it was explained that Jesus was the Lamb slain for our sin. And there was certainly nothing intentionally depressing about the advertisements for Joel and Victoria's extensive product line flashing on the enormous screens flanking the altar, Victoria's face peeking out from the pinky cover of her debut book, *Love Your Life: Living Happy, Healthy, and Whole*. She was right. It was already Easter.

I am out for dinner with two friends at our favorite dive restaurant and we should be having a lovely time except that I am ranting. I am livid about a Facebook post that read something like "Just a little life in the midst of death!" and an accompanying video testimony about a celebrity who learned that, in trusting God, she could expand her self-esteem and her business. "Trust me with your dreams," God had said to her, "and I will take your business farther than you could have imagined." People are tweeting at me about having "Joseph-sized expectations," referring to the Old Testament story about a young man who suffers before rising to positions of unimagined wealth and good fortune. Everything could be mine if I would just reach for it.

I attend a Christian conference between hospital days, and the speaker is a gorgeous thirty-something woman with shiny hair and skinny jeans. She is telling a young audience to think hard about who they have godly influence over. She looks so effortlessly perfect that she does what most female speakers do—she reaches for a self-deprecating joke. She insists that she has no luck with suburban moms ("They don't like that I never wash my hair!"), baristas ("I never get my order right!"), urban professionals ("They're so hip!"), and the dying.

"If I saw a person who was dying, I'd be like 'Shh-hhh . . . Goodbye . . . I'm so sorry . . . You're scaring me . . . '" She flashes a wide smile and she gets a big laugh in return. It is approaching Holy Week, but death is still a punch line.

I am facing death and the church has demanded that, for the forty days of Lent, everyone stare it down with me. We are solid flesh, and we are ashes.

Pulvis es, et in pulverem reverteris.

"Everyone is trying to Easter the crap out of my Lent," I say to my friends through gritted teeth and tears.

I am marching toward the edge of a precipice, trusting that, by the time I get there, a bridge will have been built. Chemotherapy. Immunotherapy. Divine healing. Something needs to happen before I get there. *Lord, build me a bridge.*

I AM SITTING ACROSS from my friend Ray, who is a pediatric oncologist, which is to say that every day he talks to children and parents about tumors and white blood cell counts and life expectancy. He is a shepherd of little lambs who are often plucked up by cancer and led to slaughter. When I look at him, I see the dogged expression of a man who fights even though he might lose. Every day he sits down with someone's mother and father and looks them directly in the eye and says: "There is hope" or "I'm sorry." He knows what it is like to explode the world.

The first time he sat on my patio like this was in the immediate aftermath of my diagnosis, when the doctors guessed I had only months to live. My house was packed to the ceiling with my family, buzzing with the exhausted energy of people trying to save the world by doing laundry and making more chicken stock. There was nothing anyone could do for me, so they did everything else. Someone was always folding linens or checking on my medication or picking up groceries to stock the freezer. My mom had bought disposable surgical masks for everyone to wear, and I spent the rest of the time trying to convince people that they didn't have to wear them. I was sitting on the patio in my cocoon of blankets when Ray popped his head over the fence with a conspiratorial grin. He was carrying two bottles of expensive wine and he poured a glass for everyone, including me, the girl with giant liver tumors who probably shouldn't be drinking anything but water. I loved him for it. He sat down beside me like we were part of the same exclusive club. And then he turned to face my parents.

"I am so sorry that this is happening," he said. "This is awful."

My parents looked at him for a moment, blinking. I think they were a little stunned.

There is a tone that professionals often take with people in crisis, and I've come to recognize it as "Hostage Negotiator Neutral." It's the sort of voice that is trying to communicate "Don't jump!" to a person on the edge, but implies that everyone in the room is mentally incapacitated. Doctors use it with me all the time. They are telling me something important, but everything about their tone and wording suggests that they are telling me a version of the truth to keep me from jumping. "We can try a few things" usually means "This is hopeless, but I think I can stretch out your decline." "We can focus on your comfort" always means "We're giving up." And no one ever, ever, ever starts with the truth.

"This is awful," Ray said again. And it was the truth, but it was strange to hear it said aloud. He pushed on relentlessly. "But let me tell you what I know."

He proceeded to tell them that there were a lot of new developments in cancer research and that it was going to require a certain mindset. We would need to prepare to think beyond "cured" and "dying" and think, instead, about how to get me from one good outcome to another. The longer he talked the more I came to recognize the look on my parents' faces. Hope.

It is why I sometimes save my tender questions for Ray, who will tell me the truth.

Now we are sitting in the same place where he once faced down my two grieving parents, and there's another open bottle of wine. It's time.

"Does it hurt to die?" I ask. "In the hospital, I mean."

He pauses.

"No . . ." he says finally. "Not really. I mean, not as much." He has already promised me that if I fight as hard as I can—if I agree to be blasted with whatever drugs and endure whatever side effects—he will make the end as comfortable as possible. I don't tell anyone that. But I think about it sometimes when I wonder how long I can bear the side effects or the needles or the look in people's eyes.

"Are you okay?" he asks.

"Yes, yes, I'm okay. Except for about ten minutes a day, I'm okay."

Anyone else would have left it at that.

He looks at me carefully. "What does it look like? Those ten minutes?" he asks.

I remember then that I am talking to someone who knows, almost as well as I do, what those ten minutes are like. He has seen those moments play out a hundred different ways. Kids who scream. Kids who beg for it to stop. Kids who hug their stuffed animals and ask for their moms to lie beside them. Teenagers who beat their pillows and ask about what it would have been like to grow up. What is true love like? What is it like to have sex? Do you think someone would have married me?

I think about his question a long time as I watch Toban and Zach across the lawn. I can see Toban taking out his wrench set to fix the lawnmower, and Zach, hopping around him, is leaking his purple Popsicle all over the equipment. Toban looks up at him, frustrated and amused.

"I know exactly how it feels," I say finally, finding it hard to take my eyes off the boys. "It feels like I'm hungry and I'll never be full again."

I SWEAR FOR ALL of Lent. Every inch of it. And then one Sunday brunch, like a fever, it breaks.

My friend Blair and I are sitting over perfectly cured bacon and eggs that float on tender southern biscuits, and she announces that her "death thoughts" are back. She is weaning herself off of antidepressants, now that things in her life are chugging along, but all the familiar worries about her mortality have resurfaced. Her dad is suffering from early-onset Alzheimer's, and the man she once knew is now confused and alien to her. But every time her memory slips she is brought back to a possible future: is this going to happen to her? She could take a genetic test and find out, but then she would have to live with the inevitability of her own decline, the prospect that she might lose decades of moments with a husband she adores and a life she has built with incredible care.

Or not.

She can't bear the answer, and I realize deep into the story that I am smiling ear to ear. I am the worst person in the world. I have wept with her about her father. I have moved furniture with her into her new house, which we can all agree is the true test of friendship. She is the reason that I own a head-to-toe Tonya Harding costume, complete with a figure-skating warm-up outfit covered in an American flag, even though there is no Halloween scenario in which anyone will ever look at me carrying a crowbar and say, "That's a great Tonya Harding costume." Blair and I have spent entire parties confusing guests by trading wigs and stayed up far too late agonizing together over failed friendships. So why am I smiling like the worst person on earth?

"I'm so sorry," I say. Blair starts to laugh. "It's not that I would ever want this for you, but—I'm sorry for saying this—but you live here too."

"What do you mean?"

"You live with an uncertain future. You live here too. And—I'm so sorry—but I'm so *fucking* grateful to have you here."

And as I start to cry over our upscale brunch, Blair starts to laugh even louder.

CHAPTER 9

Ordinary Time

EASTER HAS POURED ITSELF OUT, AND NOW WE members of the church are stumbling through what the church calendar calls "Ordinary Time," the second installment of the phase traditionally beginning with Epiphany in early January and ending with Ash Wednesday. Ordinary Time picks up again after the mysteries of Easter and Jesus' ascension into heaven have passed, and stretches out to swallow the rest of the year. It is the space between. It is a time for baptisms and weddings, teaching and preaching without the highs and lows of Jesus' cosmic interventions. Church attendance flags. There is no birth at the manger or death on the cross, just the ponderous pace of people singing, praying, and keeping their kids quiet during the sermon. The magic fades and reveals the church for what it is: a plain people in a boring building who meet until kickoff.

Time is looped. Start treatment, manage the side effects, recover, start treatment. My weekly rituals revolve around Wednesdays, when I fly to Atlanta for chemotherapy. I wake up at 4:00 A.M. and drive to the airport listening to a radio program about the wonders of the periodic table of elements, and I find myself telling Toban later: "Next week it's boron!" By 6:00 A.M. I have parked, gone through airport security, answered most of my emails, and boarded the plane to Atlanta. The same plane that will bring me back at midnight, always to the soundtrack of people coughing and a nearby baby screaming herself unconscious.

There are some interruptions to this ritual. Once I got into a lively discussion with airport security about whether their slogan should be "The customer is always wrong!" Another time a pair of crutches fell from the overhead luggage bin onto my head and, in the dark of the plane, I spent an inappropriately long time trying to figure out if I was bleeding. But normally, the day is a blur of Atlanta traffic, needles, waiting rooms, and chemo chairs, with intermittent chatter. Determined to charm the intake nurses, the blood-work nurses, and the enormous entourage of highly trained doctors who are working on this clinical trial, I wear myself out. I am starring in my own reality show about a young woman who gets cancer and is extremely cheerful about it. Except that no one is watching. By the time I crawl into bed at 1:00 A.M., I am hollow. There is nothing left, except the budding dread of knowing that next Wednesday I will do it all again.

I AM STUCK IN present tense. With a scan around every corner, I have lost the ability to make extended plans, to reach into the future and speak its language. I have lost the rhythm of anticipating the seasons. In the fall, my mom and I like to celebrate the first snow on the ground with homemade donuts, crispy apple fritters puffed up with oil and sprinkled with cinnamon and sugar. In the winter, we drive out to see Grandpa at his retirement facility in a Mennonite town a few hours away and let all the children chase each other like puppies while the adults pretend to be indifferent about losing at Ping-Pong. The spring is about grading papers near the duck ponds in Duke Gardens. The summer is a liturgy of picnics and water skiing on Ontario lakes, watching Toban's annual reminder to himself that he is eerily graceful skating across the surface of the water, and seeing him grin like the boy I met at summer camp. But the year ahead is floating away, too far to see, and I must keep myself sewn into the present with its pills, needles, and white blood cell counts.

Sometimes this ability to live in the moment feels like a gift. My pain feels connected to the pain of others somehow. I notice the look of exhaustion on the young mom's face at the grocery store and help her with her cart. I stop to talk to the homeless man sitting on the corner. I give money away more freely, less begrudgingly. I can see now how hard people work to keep it together, but the walls that keep their lives from falling apart are brittle.

And I have two months to live. Again.

I sit in a chemo chair with sixteen thousand dollars' worth of immunotherapy drugs efficiently pumping into my body through a port in my chest. These are the kinds of numbers I can't afford without insurance, and even if I could, I wouldn't be able to get the drug. The clinical trial has special access to these restricted drugs, and millions of dollars of pharmaceutical hopes and dreams are hanging on the news of how well they are performing in round after round of experimentation on people like me. The expectations are clear. Every sixty days I lie in a whirling CT machine, dye coursing through my veins, and the doctors measure whether the four plump tumors in my liver are growing. And if they are not, the doctors smile and agree to move on to the next sixty days of treatment. I live for two months, take a deep breath, and hope to start over again.

In those moments before I can hear the oncologist pull the chart with my results from the holder on the wall outside, his hand on the door handle of the office, my mind goes back to the bridge.

God, I am walking to the edge of a cliff. Build me a bridge. I need to get to the other side.

There are no new studies to assure me that anything will cure me or even keep me stable for long stretches of time. I am stepping out into the great void on the edge of what science can tell me. I just need sixty more days.

It has been ten months since my diagnosis, and at a recent appointment, my oncologist drew a little chart on a scrap of paper.

"This"—he drew a line—"is what we know so far about people like you on immunotherapy drugs."

The line surged up and then went flat.

"This"—he draws another—"is most people on chemotherapy with your condition." The line curved up and then swooped down. He draws a couple more squiggles: people who do better, people who are average, and people who do worse. He points at a spot that represents where I am that day on the graph with an average response to immunotherapy. I see it.

"So, if I weren't on immunotherapy, now is when I would have begun to die."

"Yes," he says simply.

This would be my last summer. This would be my last birthday. This would be the last month that Toban shoves his step counter in my face, kisses his biceps, and insists that he is getting fit faster than anyone in the history of step counters. This would be the last time I sit on the floor in Zach's room and swap out his clothes for the bigger box of sleepers and T-shirts. I would never see the house I grew up in again. This would begin the Great Goodbye.

"Okay," I said, "I understand."

I have tried, really tried, to make others understand. When the trial first started, yes, we had hoped that the tumors would shrivel up and disappear, and that I would simply maintain my progress with a regimen of immunotherapies. That is how I made sense of the word *incurable*. But in the intervening months, the tumors have stopped shrinking and our expectations for a full recovery have dried up. We hope instead that the tumors will not grow faster than the immunotherapies can shrink them. I need to make clear to my friends and family that I pray for reduced cancer, but that I must be grateful for what I have. I have two more months of life. *Hallelujah*.

I try to put it in a little Facebook post, that mix of sun and cloud. I am trying to clear the emotional hurdles of using the words that show up on my chart. *Palliative. Noncurative*. Or, we are hoping for a "manageable illness" in the face of no cure, but the comments section is a blurry mess of "Don't give up!" and "God bless you in your preparations." It feels impossible to translate the kernel of truth: *I'm not dying*. I am not terminal. *I am keeping vigil in the place of almost death*. I stand in the in-between where everyone must pass, but so few can remain.

I keep thinking that if my grandmother were still alive she would understand. When she was seventeen, she was diagnosed with tuberculosis, wildly contagious and incurable back then, which wormed its way into her lungs and devoured her life whole. She had been at the top of her class and preparing to be the first person in her family to turn a razor wit into a college education. Instead, she breathed in an errant bacterial strain, so her parents packed her things in a trunk and sent her away to a tall stone sanitarium so imposing that it earned the nickname Fort San.

I have seen pictures of where she was shuttered, and I imagine her, in the bloom of youth, watching from one of its windows as her life withered away. She could not have known that the young man who used to take her on his rounds driving the ice truck would not forget her. She could not have anticipated that a doctor would pioneer a way of cutting deep into the tissues of her lungs to successfully carve out the infection. And she never would have imagined that the young man with the ice truck would make Fort San his first stop on his way home from the war, scoop her up, and take her to a little bungalow he'd built only for her. She could not have predicted that her world wouldn't end in a locked white room.

She had had many recurring episodes in the hospital after her cure, times when her two baby boys were parceled out to relatives and friends for years while she was too sick to care for them and my grandfather traveled to keep the family afloat. These memories would press her into periods of intermittent sorrow, and her boys remembered these, and how she'd go into her room and turn the key. I still wear her ring, a blossom of diamond flecks, which she meant for me. If she were here, she would understand the cost of living in the in-between.

I KEEP RECEIVING LETTERS from strangers about the cost of a life that goes on.

"Forgive me, Kate," they write, "but I have the opposite problem. I can't justify my still being alive." They are growing old, gathering years, but they do not feel they are amounting to something. "It has become obvious to me that all this life is more than I deserve."

An old college professor writes from the deep of retirement. "I have seen *good, good* people die young while I, who have not been a particularly good person, go on." His losses are more than his gains. "At sixty-three," says another, "I find myself so afraid of death. I am ashamed to admit how much I want more time, but I have accomplished so little with what I've been given." And then they turn to me. "You, my dear, deserve to have taken some of my wasted years." A Buddhist promises to take on a special practice that will absorb my suffering and loan me his goodness. The world is a balance sheet. Subtract from one column, add to another, as if we could all agree to share pieces of this too-short, too-long life.

Instead, we plod along.

People in my position, I suppose, think about the ultimate future, the life everlasting.

But the first question I allowed myself to ask in the hours after being diagnosed was to my friend Frank, as Lutheran as a hot tuna dish.

"You know how God's time is different than ours . . . He sees everything, past and future, like it's in the same moment? I mean, we believe that the three members of the Trinity—Father, Son, and Holy Spirit—always existed even though we think Jesus was born at a moment in time. But he always existed in another sense?" I was rambling, tumbling over my sentences trying to get to the point. I tried again.

"But do you think that means that, when I die, I will see things from God's perspective?" *Say it. Just say it.*

"Do you think that when I die . . . I won't have to feel . . . apart?"

At this point it wasn't a question anymore. If I died, my son would never remember me, and so nothing in heaven held any interest for me. My eternal reward would have been that I missed it all. Frank folded his hands around mine and said something that, I'm sure, was both theologically rich and sound. But all I can remember now is that an old man who once lost his boy understood what I needed time to be—a connective thread that wraps us all together for eternity.

In moments like this, my prosperity friends from all my years of research know me best. If poked and prodded, they would probably agree with me that, while heaven is great, it is even better when it is enjoyed here on earth. Technically, this is all heresy. It's called an "overrealized eschatology," an exaggerated sense of what earth can reveal about the Kingdom of God. The famous Reverend Ike, pioneer of black televangelism, used to say it with a cheeky smile: "Don't wait for your pie in the sky by and by; have it now with ice cream and a cherry on top!" But I don't want ice cream, I want a world where there is no need for pediatric oncology, UNICEF, military budgets, or suicide rails on the top floors of tall buildings. The world would drip with mercy. *Thy kingdom come*, I pray, and my heart aches. And my tongue trips over the rest. *Thy will be done.*

And maybe it's one big disappointment. Before I got sick, I visited an actual enactment of what heaven would be like, sponsored by Jan and Paul Crouch, the omnipresent faces of Christian televangelism. This prosperity-preaching duo owned the Trinity Broadcasting Network and, among other things, had purchased the Holy Land Experience, a sweet and gaudy biblical theme park devoted to retelling the life of Jesus—if Jesus had lived in Orlando, Florida. I ate a snack at Esther's Banquet Hall and purchased the autobiography of Paul Crouch at the Gold, Frankincense and Myrrh gift shop. In their recent renovations, they had added a few flourishes, including a dozen cardboard cutouts of Jan Crouch, a tiny, grinning woman supporting her trademark purple beehive, pointing guests to various destinations: this way to the Sermon on the Mount at 10:45 A.M.; don't miss the Crucifixion at 3:00 P.M.

The death of Jesus was a giant bloodbath but touchingly portrayed by a man with very soulful eyes, and I did not once question why everyone around me was crying. But when the resurrection sequence began at 4:00 P.M., and cherubim and seraphim danced around the stage and solemn angels arrived to let the trumpets sound, I started to feel disappointed in the prospect of heaven. The actor playing Jesus appeared to enormous applause in a white robe with a long purple cape and a heavy gold crown, and paced the stage a few times, but then the music swelled and Jesus walked through wall-to-wall mirrors misted with the thick white plumes of a fog machine, and I realized that heaven could just be a fog machine in Orlando.

The future can seem awfully like the present. I remember standing on a windy hilltop in northern Israel with an elderly woman named Beverly, her shock of dyed red hair as fierce as the way she whispered the name of the ancient site.

"Megiddo," she said. "This is everything."

She spoke at a frantic pace as her eyes scanned the panoramic view, describing how the end-times armies would do battle below for the future of humankind. She gestured widely at the valleys at our feet.

"Megiddo," she said again. In Greek, the mountain went by its more common name, Armageddon, a by-word for the end of time. But every time the celebrity pastor we were traveling with uttered a prophecy, telling our assembly in conspiratorial tones that 2025 would bring Jesus back to earth to destroy the wicked and reward the righteous, Beverly tallied it to her life with painful specificity. It was too late. She would not live to see the world undone and remade.

"And people didn't even want to make the climb." She said it like she wanted to spit. Almost everyone was sitting comfortably in the tour buses below while she and I had made the trek up the mountain alone, her wobbly legs almost buckling by the final steps. Most of *them* were going to live to see the day, and they didn't even care. At the time I had thought: *What an odd duck.*

Traveling all this way to stand on an apocalyptic mountaintop.

Now I understand that she needed the view, her eyes casting beyond her horizon. For a minute there, she needed to live in that beautiful, terrible someday.

IT IS ALMOST SUMMER, but as I am only keeping track of my treatment calendar, it is another Wednesday in Atlanta. I am sitting in another visit to the hospital waiting for the next scan results. This is the sixth time I've done this, and it doesn't get easier. Deep breath. It's good. I have two more months to live. Again.

WHEN I WAS IN COLLEGE, I took a class in the philosophy of religion from a wonderful old scholar, long past retirement age, who had spent his life working on a lovely translation of the Bhagavad Gita, an ancient Sanskrit text that lays out many of the fundamental precepts of Hinduism. But mostly he gave us book after book about Hinduism's understanding of reincarnation, perpetual rebirth into new lives and bodies, and how it had probably already been proven by scientists. But mostly I remembered him because he lost his wife of fifty-plus years that semester, not from disease or old age, but because she was hit by a car crossing the road near our campus. He was so stooped by sadness that he had to stop teaching us, but in his last class I remember him saying that he couldn't breathe when he found her things around the house.

"I found her little sock in the washer today," he said, fat tears rolling down his leathered cheeks. And we all felt sad in that limited way of students too new to the world to know its burdens.

He had believed that her life would go on and on, but she had gone on without him. And he was here, stuck in her past.

Beverly lived in the apocalyptic future, and the scholar lived in the past. I think I believed that I was living in the center, but I rarely let my feet rest on solid ground, rooting me in the present. My eyes shifted to look for that thing just beyond, the next deadline, the next hurdle, the next plan. *That second baby is going to need his or her own room, so let's talk about renovations.* On long walks I forever roped Toban into my favorite topic: the next thing. How could we improve our lives? What should we do next? As we walked through the tall Carolina oaks on a fall trail dusted with Technicolor leaves, my mind hummed with possible futures. Always. If I were to invent a sin to describe what that was—for how I lived—I would not say it was simply that I didn't stop to smell the roses. It was the sin of arrogance, of becoming impervious to life itself. I failed to love what was present and decided to love what was possible instead.

I must learn to live in ordinary time, but I don't know how.

"THERE'S THE GRADUAL, LONG WAY up the mountain—and that's the easier way."

My oncologist is looking at me sternly, which I know is difficult for him. He's very nice, and this is the closest thing to a lecture he's ever given me.

"And then there's the steep, fast climb—and that's the harder way. You've been used to the hard way," he says.

I have grown used to being blasted with chemotherapy drugs. But that's not what he's trying to say. He knows I'm *hooked* on the hard way.

"I'd rather you kill me trying to cure me," I tell him, and there is a long silence afterward. We both know what he should say, and I'm grateful that he doesn't.

They are not trying to cure me. I'm not going to get to the top of the mountain.

He has been trying to lower my drug dosage, space things out, and ease up a little on the regimen, but he knows this is tough for me. I liked the idea that I was doing the harshest thing, that I was really getting somewhere. But now it's time for me to accept something harder: that I'm not sure I'm going to be able to do the extreme treatment much longer.

My treatment has been like a journey swinging on three vines. Two of these vines are chemotherapy drugs and one is the immunotherapy drug. I already had to stop one chemotherapy drug because I was losing all feeling in my hands and feet. Snip. And now I am thinking about cutting out the other chemotherapy drug. I'll be swinging on that one immunotherapy vine, hoping it holds me up. *Please, God, make it work.*

"So if we stop chemotherapy now and my tumors grow . . ." I say uncertainly.

"Then we can restart chemotherapy. Worst-case scenario, your tumors grow twenty percent by the next scan," he says quickly.

"But if the immunotherapy drug doesn't work, then I am going to die anyway." My voice sounds flat and matter-of-fact, even to me. "Right? I mean, the chemo drugs are already fading."

He is trying to reassure me, but I can't quite hear the words. I am staring at my hands, puffed with chemo toxins and the color of rhubarb. I have come to the end of what I know how to do. I know how to suffer. I know how to make the best of things. But I don't know how to do the most basic thing—I don't know how to stop. I want to stop taking these chemotherapy drugs, but what if that's the beginning of my decline? What if I need to keep going a little longer? How will I know when I can stop?

I AM SITTING ACROSS from the man who won a huge prize for his discovery of my particular form of cancer, the cell disorder that caused these tumors to bloom. For all his many efforts, his thousands of hours in the lab, I have brought him cupcakes. With sprinkles.

We have both, as it turns out, spent a lot of time walking up to the edges of things, and we are talking about what it means to face facts.

"I'm not sure I want to know what happens if I stop chemotherapy, but at the same time I want to get it over with," I confess. "What would you do?"

"I'd go to work," he says, and I realize the weight of what he is saying. His office is plain and sensible, which confirms something I already know about him five minutes into our conversation. He has suffered and is there to work.

In what were the worst moments of his life, he put one foot in front of the other. He tasked himself with a series of responsibilities that ultimately gave me back this year. And maybe many more. But what I loved more than anything was that he did it without knowing it would matter. He marched forward because it was the best he could do.

"We're all terminal," he says simply, and it answers my unspoken question. How do you stop? You just stop. You come to the end of yourself. And then you take a deep breath. And say a prayer. And get back to work.

I have had cancer for a full year now. I called my mom before the surgery, one year ago today.

"Frank told me the secret," I said to her. But the more my mom pressed for details, the more it was obvious that I was on a lot of exciting painkillers. And that I had forgotten the secret entirely.

I had asked him about heaven. He knew what I was asking because he always knows. Will I be connected? Will I miss everything? Will I see my son sprout up and learn the rules of Canadian football? Can I see him graduate and be launched into the world? How many times can I sit beside his bed and watch his eyes squeeze tight as we thank God for tractors and the sticks we throw into the stream near our house. These are the plans I have made. These are the hopes that are being ground into dust.

And then one day, out of the blue, I remembered what he said next.

"Don't skip to the end," he said, gently. "Don't skip to the end."

"WHAT DO YOU THINK I meant by that?" Frank said to me last week, sitting in my office. He can't remember saying it because that day was such a blur. We are marveling at a whole year gone by, a whole year that the doctors said I had a 30 percent chance of surviving.

"I think you meant that we just can't know. And that our brains fill in all the details, for good or for ill. We want to tell ourselves a story—any story—so we can get back to certainty," I reply. "You know me! I am so desperate to know what's going to happen. At least so I can prepare."

"I sound really deep," he says.

"I just need to make it to fifty. I need to make sure that kid is launched. I need to get most of my life *done*. I need to lock it down."

"But it comes undone. There are so many times in life when we think we have it locked down," he says. We are quiet again.

Plans are made. Plans come apart. New delights or tragedies pop up in their place. And nothing human or divine will map out this life, this life that has been more painful than I could have imagined. More beautiful than I could have imagined.

"Right. That's the secret—don't skip to the end," I remind myself, sheepishly wiping my face on the sleeve of my sweater.

My friend Kori, daytime pastor and nighttime comedian, has bought a subscription to an online life-enrichment course for way too much money. It seemed like such a great idea—let's get focused!—but now it sits unused in her iPhone downloads to the tune of six hundred dollars.

"Want to do my life-changing, goal-oriented online course with me?" asks Kori. She is the kind of person who owns her own portable photo booth with buckets of props so that every time she appears—*poof*—it's a party.

"But I am the worst at this stuff now! I can't make plans, and, geez, my life is already too meaningful," I protest.

"But think of all the fun we'll have creating our time management diaries and logging our hours spent watching *American Ninja Warrior*." She's right. We watch an Olympic amount of reality television. And at first the course assignments are not too bad. I give up a time-consuming game on my phone and agree to read more at night. But soon the daily tasks get down to the bones of my life, telling me to make concrete plans to improve my health this year, and then make a plan for five years from now.

"Five years?!" I text Kori. "I don't know . . . I guess my big goal is NOT TO DIE."

"What about your horrible spinach drink?" she asks.

"I can drink the horrible spinach drink."

"Great! And take your vitamins!" she chirps.

"The course keeps asking me to define my life philosophy and I'm not sure what to say. I want to communicate in my actions and my words that I'm living but I'm aware of the reality of death."

"Hmmmm . . ."

"I think it's something like 'Living Well, Grieving Well,'" I say uncertainly.

"Oh, absolutely not," she said. "That all sounds very serious and proper when you say it like that."

"Fine. 'No Living Well, Grieving Well.'"

"How about your motto should be 'Balls Out Living. Balls Out Grieving'?" she ventures.

When she says it, I love her more. She never treats me as if I'm rearranging deck chairs on the *Titanic,* or tacitly suggests I could save myself with my new juicing machine. She helps me walk the line between total passivity and supercharged heroic effort, but mostly she understands that the best thing she can do is order Canadian props for my patriotic Canadian Thanksgiving party and pray for me like a champion.

As we plug along with this life course, the assignments get harder.

"What are the goals for your primary relationships?" it asks. "What qualities do you want to foster in them? What thing do you want them to know with all their hearts?"

I write Toban's and Zach's names down on a blank sheet in my notebook and find myself circling their names with endless hearts. How can I have goals for these relationships in a future that might never come?

Exhausted, I stuff the notebook into the bottom of my bag.

But the questions are sticking to me. On long walks, in hospital waiting rooms, in moments before sleep. *What do I want to give them?* I have taken the notebook back out and scribbled a couple of words.

Compassion.

That one is for Zach. I have always wanted to raise a boy who loves the underdog, who stops for snails, who wants to know why the man outside the car window says he will work for food. I want to raise a tough softy. He will know the pain of the world but all will be better for it. He will be brave in the face of heartbreak.

For Toban, I write a word and then I shake my head. It is impossible: *joy.*

How can I ask a man who might lose his wife, the mother of his son, and his best friend since middle school to feel something close to joy? Sometimes we play a game called What Don't I Know About You? and the answer is always so specific that no one else can play. I recently learned that he had played the bass clarinet in grade seven, and I shrieked: *"How did I not know this? Who are you?"* I know everything. He knows everything. How can anything good live in the space that death would make?

As the question turns in my mind, my hand begins to scribble. The page is filling with words, ideas, little tidbits of something I wasn't sure I knew how to do anymore. I am making plans. I am living in Ordinary Time.

I can take care of Zach on a Saturday so Toban can take his dirt bike out on the back roads. I can buy him chocolates at every weird stop where my research takes me and put them by his desk. I can lay his arm on my knee while we watch television and trace tickly lines from his wrist to his elbow. I can run my hands through his hair and tell him that he is growing more inappropriately beautiful year by year and remind him of the time that he looked identical to an advertisement for sunglasses. I can tell his family and friends, quietly, that in case I don't survive, I want them to know the greatest truth about us is that I need him to be happy, remake his life, marry if he likes, and, as soon as possible, surprise himself by how hard he can laugh.

I buy him a huge sign that reads YOU ARE MY BUCKET LIST and hang it in our living room.

My little plans are crumbs scattered on the ground. This is all I have learned about living here, plodding along, and finding God. My well-laid plans are no longer my foundation. I can only hope that my dreams, my actions, my hopes are leaving a trail for Zach and

Toban, so, whichever way the path turns, all they will find is Love.

Zach is beside me in our big bed as I write these words, rolling around like a polar bear cub. After we take him out of his crib in the morning he loves to come "up up" to our loft bedroom and loll around like only two-year-olds can. It's another beautiful morning, and it's time to yell with the pitch of the coffee grinder and make him French toast. I will die, yes, but not today.

....

ABSOLUTELY NEVER SAY THIS TO PEOPLE EXPERIENCING TERRIBLE TIMES: A SHORT LIST

1. *"Well, at least . . ."*

Whoa. Hold up there. Were you about to make a comparison? At least it's not . . . what? Stage V cancer? Don't minimize.

2. *"In my long life, I've learned that . . ."*

Geez. Do you want a medal? I get it! You lived forever. Well, some people are worried that they won't, or that things are so hard they won't want to. So ease up on the life lessons. Life is a privilege, not a reward.

3. *"It's going to get better. I promise."*

Well, fairy godmother, that's going to be a tough row to hoe when things go badly.

4. *"God needed an angel."*

This one takes the cake because (a) it makes God look sadistic and needy and (b) angels are, according to Christian tradition, created from scratch. Not dead people looking for a cameo in *Ghost*. You see how confusing it is when we just pretend that the deceased return to help you find your car keys or make pottery?

5. *"Everything happens for a reason."*

The only thing worse than saying this is pretending that you know the reason. I've had hundreds of people tell me the reason for my cancer. Because of my sin. Because of my unfaithfulness. Because God is fair. Because God is unfair. Because of my aversion to Brussels sprouts. I mean, no one is short of reasons. So if people tell you this, make sure you are there when they go through the cruelest moments of their lives, and start offering your own. When someone is drowning, the only thing worse than failing to throw them a life preserver is handing them a reason.

6. *"I've done some research and . . ."*

I thought I should listen to my oncologist and my nutritionist and my team of specialists, but it turns out that I should be listening to you. Yes, please, tell me more about the medical secrets that only one flaxseed provider in Orlando knows. Wait, let me get a pen.

7. *"When my aunt had cancer . . ."*

My darling dear, I know you are trying to relate to me. Now you see me and you are reminded that terrible things have happened in the world. But guess what? That is where I live, in the valley of the shadow of death. But now I'm on vacation because I'm not in the hospital or dealing with my mess. Do I have to take my sunglasses off and join you in the saddest journey down memory lane, or do you mind if I finish my mojito?

8. *"So how are the treatments going? How are you really?"*

This is the toughest one of all. I can hear you trying to understand my world and be on my side. But picture the worst thing that has ever happened to you. Got it?

Now try to put it in a sentence. Now say it aloud fifty times a day. Does your head hurt? Do you feel sad? Me too. So let's just see if I want to talk about it today because sometimes I do and sometimes I want a hug and a recap of *American Ninja Warrior*.

....

GIVE THIS A GO,
SEE HOW IT WORKS:
A SHORT LIST

1. *"I'd love to bring you a meal this week. Can I email you about it?"*

Oh, thank goodness. I am starving, but mostly I can never figure out something to tell people that I need, even if I need it. But really, bring me anything. Chocolate. A potted plant. A set of weird erasers. I remember the first gift I got that wasn't about cancer and I was so happy I cried. Send me funny emails filled with You-Tube clips to watch during chemotherapy. Do something that suits your gifts. But most important, *bring me presents*!

2. *"You are a beautiful person."*

Unless you are of the opposite gender and used to speaking in a creepy windowless-van kind of voice, comments like these go a long way. Everyone wants to know they are doing a good job without feeling like they are learning a lesson. So tell your friend something about his life that you admire without making it feel like a eulogy.

3. *"I am so grateful to hear about how you're doing and just know that I'm on your team."*

You mean I don't have to give you an update? You asked someone else for all the gory details? *Whew.* Great! Now I get to feel like you are both informed and concerned. So don't gild the lily. What you have said is amazing, so don't screw it up now by being a Nosy Nellie. Ask a question about any other aspect of my life.

4. *"Can I give you a hug?"*

Some of my best moments with people have come with a hug or a hand on the arm. People who are suffering often—not always—feel isolated and want to be touched. Hospitals and big institutions in general tend to treat people like cyborgs or throwaways. So ask if your friend feels up for a hug and give her some sugar.

5. *"Oh, my friend, that sounds so hard."*

Perhaps the weirdest thing about having something awful happen is the fact that no one wants to hear about it. People tend to want to hear the summary but they don't usually want to hear it from you. And that it was awful. So simmer down and let them talk for a bit. Be willing to stare down the ugliness and sadness. Life is absurdly hard, and pretending it isn't is exhausting.

6. ******Silence******

The truth is that no one knows what to say. It's awkward. Pain is awkward. Tragedy is awkward. People's weird, suffering bodies are awkward. But take the advice of one man who wrote to me with his policy: Show up and shut up.

A FINAL PUBLIC SERVICE ANNOUNCEMENT TO SUFFERING PEOPLE:

Just remember that if cancer or divorce or tragedies of all kinds don't kill you, people's good intentions will. Take the phrase "but they mean well . . ." as your cue to run screaming from the room. Or demand presents.

You deserve a break.

ACKNOWLEDGMENTS

....

People like to assume that medicine keeps you alive, but I'm fairly certain it is writing and the people who let you write about them.

My family and friends remade the world, as far as I'm concerned. Thank you to my Bowlers and my Penners for setting aside everything to pray, cook, tend, and toddler-wrangle. And thank you to my besties who flew to North Carolina and pretended that, no big deal, they were going to visit anyway.

Thank you to Duke Divinity School, you Methodist sweethearts. You were there every step of the way.

I will never forget my superheroes in Atlanta who volunteered to feed me, house me, and take me to my weekly appointments before they had even met me. Between you and my medical team at Emory, I was in such good hands.

Greg and Susan Jones, Will and Patsy Willimon, and Grant and Kathy Wacker, you won't admit it but your efforts saved my life. If you want any of my uncompromised organs, they are yours.

I wasn't sure I could muster the effort and clarity to write a book like this, stuck as I am in the eternal present of cancer. But a few special people gave my ideas a future. Margaret Feinberg and Jessica Richie sat on my living room floor with dreams for me I could not have conjured alone. Lauren Winner, Jessica Goudeau, and the folks at the Collegeville Institute in Minnesota gave me the encouragement and structure to do more than cry into my laptop. And Zoë Pagnamenta, my agent, and Hilary Redmon, my editor, somehow knew what to keep and what to throw away. I was so fortunate to be improved by them and the team at Random House.

And, finally, my dear Toban, thank you. You are etched in every memory. If I could, I would stay with you forever.

Everything
Happens
for a Reason

Kate Bowler

A READER'S
GUIDE

Everything Happens
for a Reason
Questions and Topics
for Discussion

1. The title of the book, *Everything Happens for a Reason (And Other Lies I've Loved)*, plays on a phrase often said in an attempt to comfort those in need. What are some other popular phrases you have heard or used to respond to a friend going through a hard time?

2. The prosperity gospel, a system of belief that corresponds strength of faith with material or personal gain, is often contrasted with the simplicity and frugality taught in the Mennonite faith. Describe how strands of faith practices may have informed your experience of loss, suffering, or pain. Which aspects of these faith practices have been the most harmful? The most helpful?

3. Think about a time when you experienced a difficult situation (illness, divorce, death in the family, job

loss). What do you wish your friends and family had said to you then? What do you wish they would have done for you?

4.   What accounts for the differences between the way the congregants of a prosperity gospel church and those of a Mennonite church react to Kate's diagnosis and illness?

5.   Discuss the nature of grief, both in the book and in your own experience. What are your go-to ways to process (or avoid) grief?

6.   What unique truths emerged in *Everything Happens for a Reason* to you? In what ways does this book enhance the themes of suffering, love, grace, and redemption featured in Kate's research on the prosperity gospel?

7.   If Kate's husband, Toban, or her best friends or her parents had written this memoir, what might they have said about Kate's victories and her suffering?

8.   How does Kate's spiritual life change during the course of the book? Describe any shifts you've noticed in your own spiritual practice during a difficult period.

9. Kate writes an op-ed for the *New York Times* and receives hundreds of letters from readers expressing their own fears and grief. Why do you think these readers felt compelled to write to Kate, a stranger? What knowledge or connection do these readers seek?

10. In Chapter 7, Kate writes, "The pain of the world is being calculated, and according to some, compassion can be doled out only by the teaspoon" (page 109). How can you dole out more compassion to yourself today? To your loved ones?

11. "How can anything good live in the space that death would make" (page 164)? *Everything Happens for a Reason* is a story to comprehend a paradoxical life and faith; God is good, yet God permits suffering. Mothers beg for the lives of their children to be spared, yet children die. How does Kate make sense of a seemingly paradoxical reality? How does your faith inform how you conceive of a life of both suffering and joy?

12. In recounting her daily ten minutes of honesty to Ray, the pediatric oncologist, Kate describes those minutes as "feel[ing] like I'm hungry and I'll never be full again" (page 138). Who is someone in your life who you

go to for your ten minutes of honesty? What is it about them makes them "your person"?

13. The words of strangers who write Kate suggest that the "world is a balance sheet" (page 149) and we can subtract from and add to the abstract columns of mutual wellbeing. How do the people surrounding Kate (her husband, child, family, friends, doctors, coworkers, acquaintances) add to or subtract from her wellbeing? How are the those in your own life doing this for you?

14. "The future can seem awfully like the present" Kate writes (page 152). In what ways does Kate's present inform her ideas of the future, and vice versa? Do you find yourself living in the past, present, or future? What beauty and harm do you find when you reflect too much on the past? On the present? On the future?

15. "Don't skip to the end" (page 160). Kate's friend Frank gives her this advice on her diagnosis day. What do we lose when we assume the inevitability of our fate?

KATE BOWLER is an associate professor at Duke Divinity School. A graduate of Yale Divinity School and Duke University, Bowler is the author of *Blessed: A History of the American Prosperity Gospel* and *The Preacher's Wife: Women and Power in American Megaministry.* She lives in North Carolina with her husband and son.

katebowler.com
Facebook.com/katecbowler
Twitter: @KatecBowler
Instagram: @katecbowler